Real World Treatment Planning

A Workbook About Mental Health
Documentation and Reimbursement
Compliance Issues

Daniel W. Johnson
Stephanie J. Johnson

*Behavioral Health Management
Systems, LLC*

THOMSON

BROOKS/COLE

Australia • Canada • Mexico • Singapore • Spain • United Kingdom • United States

THOMSON

BROOKS/COLE

Executive Editor: Lisa Gebo
Assistant Editor: Alma Dea Michelena
Editorial Assistant: Sheila Walsh
Marketing Manager: Caroline Concilla
Marketing Assistant: Mary Ho
Advertising Project Manager: Tami Strang
Production Editor: Stephanie Zunich
Print Buyer: Jessica Reed

Permissions Editor: Sue Ewing
Production Service: Mary Deeg, Buuji, Inc.
Text Designer: Vernon Boes
Copy Editor: Alan DeNiro, Buuji, Inc.
Cover Designer: Andy Norris
Compositor: Buuji, Inc.
Printer: Phoenix Color Corp.

Printed in the United States of America

1 2 3 4 5 6 7 06 05 04 03 02

For more information about our products,
contact us at:
Thomson Learning Academic Resource Center
1-800-423-0563
For permission to use material from this text,
contact us by:
Phone: 1-800-730-2214
Fax: 1-800-730-2215
Web: http://www.thomsonrights.com

Library of Congress Control Number: 2002104362

ISBN 0-534-59679-7

Brooks/Cole–Thomson Learning
511 Forest Lodge Road
Pacific Grove, CA 93950
USA

Asia
Thomson Learning
5 Shenton Way #01-01
UIC Building
Singapore 068808

Australia
Nelson Thomson Learning
102 Dodds Street
South Melbourne, Victoria 3205
Australia

Canada
Nelson Thomson Learning
1120 Birchmount Road
Toronto, Ontario M1K 5G4
Canada

Europe/Middle East/Africa
Thomson Learning
High Holborn House
50/51 Bedford Row
London WC1R 4LR
United Kingdom

Latin America
Thomson Learning
Seneca, 53
Colonia Polanco
11560 Mexico D.F.
Mexico

Spain
Paraninfo Thomson Learning
Calle/Magallanes, 25
28015 Madrid, Spain

Dedicated to
Licia Louvier Johnson and Melko Anthony Jurisich

Contents

CHAPTER 15

Initial Treatment Plans   153

CHAPTER 16

Forms   161

Preface

Writing treatment plans is difficult. The truth is that many behavioral health professionals have never been taught the "why and how" of treatment planning, let alone how the world of reimbursement affects clinical documentation. Generations of mental health professionals have struggled with treatment planning, and they simply passed on what they learned as "the way we do treatment planning."

After years of consulting in behavioral health settings and watching professionals struggle to write effective treatment plans, we felt it was time to write a guide that simplified the process of writing effective treatment plans. Many other books have been written on treatment planning, but this workbook was written specifically to meld the art of meeting Medicare standards and teaching professionals to write effective care plans.

Meeting Medicare standards is more than addressing the federal guidelines and clinical standards for providing mental health care. The Medicare standards were written by a team of professionals who tried to clinically define the art of writing a good treatment plan. Their intent was to ensure that the patient gets what he or she needs out of treatment—and they succeeded. Additionally, the Medicare standards for clinical records apply to *all patients* who receive care from medical providers who accept Medicare and Medicaid as payment for their services.

When we sent out the initial book prospectus for review, the response was overwhelmingly along the lines of, "Our students need an effective book to teach the art of treatment planning." In order to survive in today's reimbursement environment, it is not enough to provide good care. Many accrediting bodies, governmental agencies, and insurance companies play a huge role in the therapy we provide; indeed, in our continued ability to provide care. This workbook will help you meet the needs of these various entities.

This workbook introduces the reader to the history of reimbursement changes in the United States and why treatment plans have become so critical to managing patients in the current fiscal and regulatory environment. Moreover, this workbook will serve as a guide to help behavioral health professionals write mental health care plans that improve their client's quality of care and patient outcomes.

This workbook is not intended to be a scholarly text on the use of, or benefits regarding, various therapeutic approaches to treatment. Neither is it written to promote any specific therapeutic school of thought. This workbook is designed to provide mental health professionals with a hands-on approach to writing behavioral care plans and to improve the documentation in patient records. It is written in basic terms and provides many useful forms that will help you meet the requirements of varied regulatory bodies and provide good care as well.

ACKNOWLEDGMENTS

We would like to thank the following individuals for their kind guidance and suggestions. Their reviews and input was invaluable in making *Real World Treatment Planning* a better book.

Michael Altekruse, University of North Texas
Marcia Harrigan, Virginia Commonwealth University
Dona Kennealley, University of South Dakota
Craig LeCroy, Arizona State University
Jackie Leibsohn, Seattle University
Gordon MacNeil, University of Alabama
Tommy Milford, Southern Arkansas University

*How do you know when you get there . . . if you
don't know where you are going?*

Introduction

This age-old question is the essence of treatment planning. A treatment plan is the map that guides successful patient treatment in a coordinated continuum of care.

WHY DO PEOPLE SEEK TREATMENT?

People seek treatment when they become overwhelmed and lack the capacity to deal with their problems. The patient seeks help from treatment professionals, expecting that the therapist or physician will be able to help him or her sort out the problems faced and teach self-reliance in solving problems.

What Is a Treatment Plan?

A treatment plan is a therapeutic road map to help patients improve their mental health and daily functioning. In its simplest form, this plan will help the patient resolve enough problems so that he or she can function at a higher level and move to a less restrictive treatment environment. Therapy is almost never a short-term process. Mental health professionals use a multitude of settings and a variety of modalities to help the patient recover. As the patient gets better, the intensity and focus of these settings and modalities decrease. Therefore, the patient can step down to a lower, less intensive level of care. This step-down process moves the patient through a continuum of care until he or she can function at the highest possible level in the least restrictive environment possible. A good treatment plan will coordinate the patient's movement throughout the entire continuum of care.

What Is a Continuum of Care?

All patients go through a progression of recovery. When a patient first seeks help, the treating mental health professional has to make a determination about placement in the correct therapeutic environment. The most restrictive environment is a hospital setting. Generally, very stringent admission criteria govern inpatient mental health admissions. Patients must be a danger to themselves, others, or be gravely disabled. "Gravely disabled" means a patient is unable to carry out activities of daily living.

These "commitment criteria" are usually universally accepted admission criteria. In other words, the patient must exhibit need for nursing and medical interventions in a safe environment 24 hours a day, 7 days a week.

Not all patients require this kind of treatment. Some clients would do well in a partial or outpatient treatment program. The intensity of the problems and the focus of treatment interventions will determine where the patient fits on the treatment continuum. *Note: The use of the terms "clients" and "patients" are interchangeable based on therapist preference. Most often outpatients are referred to as clients, but, for the purpose of this text, the terms are used interchangeably.*

Figure 1.1 shows an example of a treatment continuum. It begins with the most restrictive treatment environment and progresses to less restrictive programs. As the need for continuous intervention decreases, the staff can focus on helping the patient function in an environment that is more homelike. For instance, in the hospital, the focus of treatment may be on protecting a patient who has command suicidal hallucinations. However, in a partial program, the focus of treatment might be to increase work activities after the patient has become stable. The staff is managing the same problem, but is using a different focus and intensity of treatment. Also, the less restrictive forms of treatment are usually less expensive. Resource conservation plays a huge role in treatment decisions.

Once the treating professional makes a determination about what treatment environment best suits the patient, treatment can begin. As the patient gets better, the staff can move him or her to a less restrictive treatment environment. If the behavior or condition worsens, the patient will require a more intense, controlled environment.

How a patient moves up and down a progressively restrictive scale of treatment environments—that is, through the continuum of care—depends on the severity of the patient's problems. Choosing the right mental health treatment environment and changing the focus of treatment based on the patient's progress is necessary to help him or her function independently in the environment that most closely matches his or her home environment.

This text will deal with problem acuity scales and the focus of treatment in Chapter 12, but for now, remember that patients have the right to as much freedom in treatment as their conditions allow.

Why Write Treatment Plans?

Anyone who has ever been in a hospital can empathize with the helplessness and confusion that a patient feels.

Doctors, nurses, and medical professionals bustle in and out of the patient's room providing constant monitoring and care. Because healthcare changes have resulted in decreased staffing, medical professionals may be too harried to stop and explain each procedure to each patient, even though hospital protocols require patient instruction. When they do not take time to explain what's going on with the patient's treatment, they have forgotten the most basic element of care—the patient!

Mental health patients, in particular, are extremely vulnerable and must be aware of their plan of care. The following principles are necessary to carry out successful treatment:

1. Patients should know what problems their treatment plan will address.
2. Patients should know how each member of their treatment team plans to help them resolve their problems.

Figure 1.1 | Continuum of Care

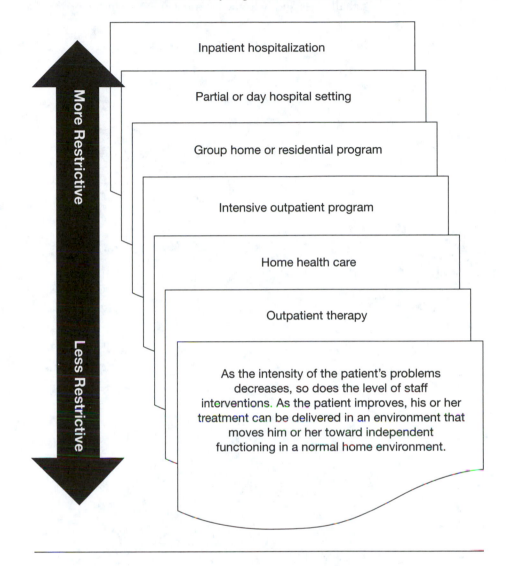

Although this graph depicts the most restrictive environment first, treatment usually begins in the least restrictive environment.

More Restrictive

Less Restrictive

Inpatient hospitalization

Partial or day hospital setting

Group home or residential program

Intensive outpatient program

Home health care

Outpatient therapy

As the intensity of the patient's problems decreases, so does the level of staff interventions. As the patient improves, his or her treatment can be delivered in an environment that moves him or her toward independent functioning in a normal home environment.

3. Patients should know what treatment modalities (i.e., medications, group therapy, activities therapy, family therapy, etc.) will be utilized to deal with their problems and how often they will be expected to participate in these forms of treatment.
4. Patients should understand the expected outcomes of their treatment.
5. Both patients and their treatment team must understand and participate in the formulation and implementation of the patients' individualized treatment plan.

These are the basic elements of good treatment planning. Patients need to feel that the mental health professionals who provide care can help them sort out their problems and teach new, healthy ways to deal with issues.

Patients must be integrally involved in their own recovery. In order to accomplish this; the therapist or team must have a concise, well-organized plan to resolve patient problems. The task of writing and implementing a meaningful and effective treatment plan is difficult enough by itself.

However, as you will soon learn, government agencies, insurance regulations, financial considerations and accreditation organizations make the task of planning and documenting good care even more challenging.

This workbook will help students and professionals learn to meet these challenges and help their patients recover in the process.

CHAPTER 1 SELF-TEST

Answer the following questions. When you have completed the test, check your answers in Appendix B.

1. What causes patients to seek mental health care?

2. What is a treatment plan?

3. What are the five principles of successful treatment planning?

4. Who is responsible for formulating a treatment plan?

5. Define a continuum of care.

The whole imposing edifice of modern medicine is like the celebrated Tower of Pisa . . . slightly off balance. — **Charles, Prince of Wales**

Real World Scenarios

Like it or not, health care is big business and someone has to pay the bill.

WHO PAYS FOR MENTAL HEALTH CARE?

Before we examine the clinical side of treatment planning, it is imperative to understand the issues that financially direct the delivery of healthcare services along the continuum of care. There is an old saying: "Money is not the most important thing, but it buys whatever comes in second place," and unfortunately, this is true in health care today.

Insurance companies provide most of the financing for mental health care in America. Only the very wealthy can afford to pay "out of pocket" for treatment. The rest of America relies on private insurance, Medicare, or Medicaid to pay for health care.

The Healthcare Triumvirate

The issue of paying for health care affects three groups of people: the insurance companies and the patient, who are both concerned about how much they pay (but for very different reasons); and healthcare providers, who are concerned with how much they are going to get paid for rendering services. All of these groups are dependent on each other for survival, but have very different ideas about the purpose of their existence.

Building a Hospital Does Not Mean You Can Treat a Patient!

For many patients in need of critical healthcare services, the first stop is the hospital. Let us first review the payment process from a hospital-based perspective.

Anyone can build a hospital, staff it, and take care of patients, but they cannot receive payments for their services without a state license. The hospital must apply for and meet certain requirements to obtain a state license. Getting licensed is just the beginning, because obtaining a license to operate a hospital does not mean that insurance companies will pay for the services it provides. Medicare and private insurance companies require another step or two before they will pay for the care a hospital provides.

The hospital's financial goal is to be able to treat the largest segment of the healthcare market, therefore it is necessary to apply for Medicare certification. The Centers for Medicare and Medicaid Services, or CMS manages the certification process for Medicare. CMS uses a survey process to certify that a provider hospital and its staff meets the qualifications and requirements to treat patients under the Medicare and Medicaid programs. Since this represents a large portion of healthcare insurance coverage in America, Medicare and Medicaid certification can mean the difference between financial viability and a hospital closing its doors.

After a hospital receives certification to treat Medicare and Medicaid patients, most private insurance companies require another survey/certification process before they will pay for care. The Joint Commission on Accreditation of Health Care Organizations, or JCAHO, manages this certification process, called "accreditation." Therefore, in order to capture a share of the private insurance market, hospitals seek accreditation by JCAHO.

Medicare and JCAHO also accredit a large number of providers in various nonhospital settings. This accreditation/certification is a precursor to reimbursement in these environments as well.

JCAHO accreditation provides an additional benefit for hospitals. Ordinarily hospitals must go through the CMS survey process every year. However, as long as hospitals maintain accreditation in good standing with JCAHO, they receive a "deemed status" with CMS. This means that a hospital that is JCAHO accredited is deemed qualified to meet the standards for Medicare certification *except* in the case of mental health services. To treat mental health patients, hospitals must meet the special conditions of participation. These additional CMS standards can be found in the Appendix of this workbook.

The Battle to Control Healthcare Costs

Employers usually provide their employees with health insurance as a benefit of employment. Employees and employers share the cost of healthcare insurance. However, employers usually pay the majority of the cost for healthcare benefits, so the employers usually negotiate with insurance companies to administer their insurance benefits. Because employers control the purse strings, they decide what kind of healthcare services they will pay for. They also determine "how much" and "how long" they are willing to pay for those services.

Over the past several decades, private insurance companies have reduced coverage for psychiatric care.

The term "coverage" delineates the scope of services that will be reimbursed and the amount of money that will be paid for those services.

Twenty years ago, it was commonplace to find individuals with $1 million psychiatric policies. Consequentially, patients regularly stayed in mental settings for months or even years.

Private insurance companies fought to hold down the spiraling cost of mental health care. They focused their attention on the rapidly expanding private "freestanding" psychiatric hospitals by excluding payment for services in a variety of ingenious and sometimes devious ways. This in turn caused providers to come up with even more devious countermeasures to protect their turf. Both sides were so wrapped up in fighting for their profits that patient treatment began to suffer. Finally, the insurance industry turned to managed care to solve their problems. The truth is, both sides were wrong. The insurance companies were wrong for denying payment singularly based on cost-containment issues and the treatment providers were not able to adequately document the patient's need for psychiatric care, thus weakening their case for reimbursement. This tangled web of stratagems can be summed up by acknowledging that although flawed, managed care exists because prior systems of providing care failed to contain costs, and provide access to those who need services.

Employers, who had been staggered by the rising cost of psychiatric care, were quick to jump on the managed care bandwagon. Right or wrong, two perceptions of mental health care crystallized:

> Psychiatric and drug abuse patients stayed in the hospital until their benefits (coverage) ran out.

> Although psychiatric patients stayed in hospitals for months and insurance companies funded tens of millions of dollars for psychiatric care, the patients did not get well.

As a result, insurance companies stopped trying to regulate the quality or types of psychiatric care provided. In fact, they were skeptical that behavioral health providers could deliver quality care, period. Instead, insurance companies did one of three things:

1. They "carved out" (separately managed) mental health benefits, and limited the dollar amounts paid for mental heath treatment. *(Mental health carve-outs cover 149 million Americans, of whom 90 million are covered by three large companies: Magellan Health Services, Value Behavioral Health, and United Behavioral Health, according to the Alliance for Health Reform.)*
2. They severely limited access to behavioral health services.
3. They stopped paying for behavioral health services.

The logic was simple. Patients could receive whatever care they wanted, wherever they wanted it, but when the money was gone, *it was gone.* This system of managing mental health benefits has become the standard for the private insurance sector.

MEDICAID AND MEDICARE

The Centers for Medicare and Medicaid Services, or CMS, (formally known as the Healthcare Financing Administration, or HCFA) is the U.S. government agency that oversees the payment for and quality of the Medicare and Medicaid programs (Title XVIII and XIX of the Social Security Act). The Medicare program provides medical care for the elderly or disabled, and Medicaid helps people who cannot afford health services. Medicare and Medicaid benefits have evolved over time, and now cover many health benefits that did not exist at the inception of the programs. As the field of medicine has progressed, the things that Medicare and Medicaid pays for has increased. This increase in coverage for new therapies and treatments is a part of the upward spiral of healthcare costs and budget overruns for CMS.

The Medicaid Program

The Medicaid program pays for the care received by the vast majority of chronic and indigent mental health patients in America. Federal and state governments jointly fund and oversee the Medicaid program. In most situations, CMS augments the amount of money paid for Medicaid through the use of matching funds. For every dollar a state budgets for Medicaid, the federal government matches that amount in various percentages.

Most chronic mental patients cannot work. Since they are unable to work, they do not have access to private insurance. Medicaid patients must prove financial need or disability. They are required to expend almost all of their resources before they become eligible to apply for Medicaid coverage. When the patient finally does become eligible for services, he or she has usually deteriorated to the point of being severely ill.

Community mental health centers manage the care provided to most chronic and indigent psychiatric patients. Patients receive ongoing services and see a variety of mental health professionals who coordinate their care. If a patient dramatically deteriorates, there are a limited number of inpatient psychiatric treatment services covered by Medicaid.

The Medicare Program

The U.S. government administers the Medicare program. The primary purpose of the program is to provide healthcare benefits to those individuals who are elderly or disabled.

Most often, Medicare and Medicaid programs serve different patient populations. They are separate programs with different funding sources; however, they do have one major common denominator, CMS.

Centers for Medicare and Medicaid Services

CMS is responsible for insuring that treatments paid for with federal funding meet certain standards. Unlike private insurance payers, CMS *is* integrally involved in the type and quality of treatment services that Medicare and Medicaid patients receive.

As stated earlier, before hospitals can accept and treat Medicare patients, they must undergo a compliance survey and receive CMS certification. All providers must meet certain standards in order to receive payment for the care they provide to Medicare and Medicaid patients. CMS checks behavioral health services on a regular basis to monitor the care patients receive. These regular checks are "compliance surveys." Behavioral health providers that fail compliance surveys could lose their CMS certification. When a provider loses its CMS certification, it can no longer treat Medicare and Medicaid patients.

Usually, when a *hospital* is decertified (loses its certification) by CMS, it comes under intense scrutiny from state licensing agencies and, if it is accredited, the Joint Commission on Accreditation of Health Care Organizations.

CMS is the largest health insurance provider in America and it has demanding expectations regarding the care patients receive. In fact, CMS has the highest standard of care for psychiatric patients in America.

Special Conditions of Participation for Psychiatric Hospitals

Hospitals that choose to treat Medicare behavioral health patients are subject to additional scrutiny from CMS. In order to care for Medicare and Medicaid funded behavioral health patients, hospitals must pass three additional tests called conditions of participation. (A copy of the clinical records standards for CMS is provided in the Appendix of this workbook.)

SPECIAL CONDITIONS OF PARTICIPATION

1. Hospitals must meet special staffing standards.
2. Hospitals must be in compliance with special conditions for managing their medical records. (*This standard of care primarily deals with treatment planning. CMS regulations state that each patient must receive an individualized treatment plan.*)
3. Hospitals must be in compliance with stringent discharge planning criteria. (*CMS introduced this condition of participation in 1995. The organization recognized that hospital stays were getting shorter and that preparing a patient to move to another, lower level of care was a critical piece of the plan for care.*)

CMS provides more payments for mental health services than anyone in the United States. Additionally, laws prohibit discrimination based on a person's ability to pay for treatment, or based on his or her type of insurance. Therefore,

CMS standards apply to all mental health patients in behavioral health treatment, regardless of their type of insurance!

Because all patients must receive the same level of care and CMS has the highest standard of care,

CMS conditions of participation for behavioral health providers dictates the standard for treatment planning *for all psychiatric patients*.

When a Medicare surveyor comes into a facility to do a compliance survey, he or she will not ask for medical records for only Medicare and Medicaid patients, but will ask to review *all charts*.

THE BOTTOM LINE IS THE BOTTOM LINE

In the real world, people do not work for free. Therefore, the golden rule of funding applies.

Providing psychiatric treatment is expensive. If providers expect payment for treating mental health patients in the United States, they need to become very familiar with CMS guidelines for treatment planning.

It is important to note that not all insurance companies require or even want the same documentation required by CMS, but many accrediting bodies are following suit with CMS. Keep in mind there will be many situations where funding sources, treatment regulations, and even accrediting agencies will contradict one another. It is important to be flexible and to include the required documentation for all parties, although this will require some inventive processes.

CHAPTER 2 SELF-TEST

Answer the following questions. When you have completed the test, check your answers in Appendix B.

1. What does the term *insurance coverage* mean?

2. What are three conditions of participation in the Medicare psychiatric program?

3. What are two common perceptions of mental health treatment that led to managed care?

4. Who usually shares the cost of employee health benefits?

5. What does CMS stand for and what is its role in health care?

6. What does JCAHO stand for?

An intelligent plan is the first step to success. The man who plans knows where he is going, knows what progress he is making, and has a pretty good idea when he will arrive. — **Basil S. Walsh**

The Advantages of a Treatment Plan | 3

Where no plan has been laid, time will soon be surrendered to chaos.

IS A TREATMENT PLAN WASTED PAPER?

Therapists seem to have great difficulty writing effective, meaningful, and individualized treatment plans for patient care. They usually explain this phenomenon as follows:

> "Treatment plans are just something we have to write to make the surveyors happy. We really do not use them for anything."

> "If therapists spent all their time writing treatment plans, there would not be any time left to take care of their patients."

First, a good treatment plan is the roadmap for effective treatment. A good plan will help the staff determine what problems prevent the patient from moving to a less restrictive environment for care.

Second, a treatment plan will force the staff to determine which therapeutic interventions will most effectively help the patient muster his or her resources and deal with those problems.

> **The paradox is this: How can mental health professionals "take care of a patient" when no one has taken the time to think about what care the patient needs? Without a unified and coordinated plan for care, any attempt to treat a patient leaves recovery to chance.**

How Long Does it Take to Do a Good Plan of Care?

An average treatment plan takes between 30–45 minutes. Is that too much time to spend planning the care of a patient?

Absolutely not!

A good treatment plan helps the treatment team stay focused on relevant problems and presents a consistent, united approach for dealing with treatment issues. In the long run, a consistent, well-written plan of care will decrease unnecessary therapeutic effort, improve treatment team coordination, and advance the purpose and focus of therapeutic interventions. In other words, rather than waste time, writing a good plan will significantly improve the amount of quality time a patient receives.

Writing a Good Plan Is Tough

Treatment planning is difficult and there are many reasons why treatment professionals fail to write good treatment plans.

To paraphrase Walt Disney, people fail for two reasons:

1. They do not understand what is expected of them.
2. They do not have the resources to accomplish their tasks.

Many mental health professionals have never learned to write treatment plans. Additionally, since managed care has brought about shorter lengths of stay and less staff, treatment time has become a very valuable commodity. Therefore, mental health professionals cannot afford to waste time doing ineffective treatment.

Everyone Wins!

With a useful treatment plan, everyone involved in the process gains a distinct advantage in treatment. A good treatment plan is a win–win situation for everyone. Here are some of the rewards of taking the time and effort to produce a meaningful plan.

The Patient

The patient receives treatment that is relevant, individualized, and focused. A treatment plan is a cooperative agreement between a patient and his or her treatment team to deal with specific issues. Some distinct benefits for the patient are:

1. The patient can be assured that a holistic approach was used to develop his or her plan of care, based on a synthesis of the treatment team's assessments and a diagnosis that is substantiated as a result of those assessments.
2. The patient and his or her treatment team will mutually develop a plan for care. The team will specifically choose to address certain "active" problems. These disabilities are usually the problems that directly prompted the current episode of care. Other problems, not directly related to the current psychiatric episode, should be "deferred" until a later time or treatment in a less restrictive treatment setting.
3. The patient will understand the goals of his or her treatment and know what he or she must accomplish before being moved to a lower level of care.
4. Each problem will have a specific set of therapeutic interventions. CMS standards require each intervention to contain four specific types of information. The required information is as follows:

   - The patient will know the name and discipline of the member of the treatment team who is primarily responsible for ensuring the completion of the treatment intervention.
   - The patient will understand what treatment modality the team will use to address each problem.

- The patient will know the focus of each therapy attended. This means that the patient will understand why he or she goes to specific therapies and what the results should be.
- The patient will know the frequency of the treatment interventions or modalities; that is, how often he or she should attend.

CMS and JCAHO focus their surveys to ensure active, individualized treatment. They check to be certain that the patient understands why he or she is going to a specific group, and what the patient is supposed to accomplish by attending that treatment activity.

For years, treatment facilities have created therapeutic schedules that encompass a plethora of treatment approaches and modalities. Patients follow the schedule with a religious fervor. In many cases, patients are clueless about the purpose of specific groups and therapeutic activities. When patients are asked why they go to group, they answer, "Because it is nine o'clock, and that is when we have group."

In some behavioral health settings, group and therapeutic activities have become a series of "time filling" or "babysitting" activities. A good plan for care returns the therapeutic purpose to therapy.

In summary, a good treatment plan will help the patient and therapist understand the planned treatment objectives. The plan will ensure that patient and therapist will have a cooperative plan to resolve problems. A good plan will make certain the patient has a therapeutic reason to attend activities and groups, and that the treatment team knows what they should be helping the patient achieve in these therapeutic processes.

The Treatment Team

Good treatment plans will create greater clarity and purpose for the therapist or treatment team. Each problem will have a specific plan for resolution and each staff member will be aware of his or her specific role in making treatment successful. The lines of communication are open.

As the patient's treatment progresses, or fails to progress, changes are made to the plan as necessary. The treatment plan becomes a living document that grows and shifts according to the patient's needs.

The Treatment Facility

Treatment facilities are coming under increased legal, financial, and clinical scrutiny. In the real world of mental health treatment, documentation is the key to survival.

There is an old axiom that almost all health providers learn early in their careers. It does not matter how much you did for the patient:

If it isn't documented, it wasn't done.

This is sage wisdom. The medical record is a legal document. Without proper documentation, you have no legal protection against litigation.

Often, staff will tell you, "I give wonderful care, but I just don't have time to write it down." Unsubstantiated claims *will not prevail,* either in a court of law, or during a survey. Document it!

The treatment facility, as well as the patients and staff, benefit from improved treatment planning. The result is an overall improvement in the facility (see Fig. 3.1).

Figure 3.1 | The Results of Improved Treatment Planning

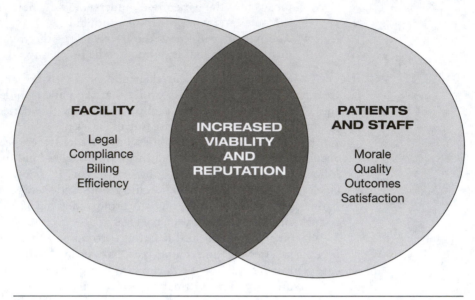

Treatment facility benefits include:

a. Improved documentation to be able to deal with legal issues. In an increasingly litigious environment, good documentation can be the best safeguard against legal action.
b. Improved documentation to help assure compliance with accreditation and licensing requirements.
c. Documentation that justifies and verifies the bill for treatment. Accountability reviews of clinical charting are increasing. Insurance companies deny claims based on improper documentation.
d. The staff understands treatment expectations and the plan to achieve them.

Patient and staff benefits include:

a. An increased sense of achievement and purpose.
b. Better care that increases the facility reputation for quality of care.
c. Better planning and coordination to improve treatment outcomes.
d. Better results and coordination to improve the quality of care and increase patient and family satisfaction.

In summary, the treatment facility will experience a multitude of positive changes, including increased viability and improved reputation.

The Insurance Companies

Insurance companies will also benefit from good documentation and the improved results that follow good treatment planning.

For years, one of the major complaints about psychiatric care was lack of results. Well-planned treatment assures improved documentation and results. Insurance reviewers will be able to review the patient's progress based on behavioral and measurable objectives.

Chart audits will more accurately reflect the care provided and treatment outcomes measured. Utilization reviewers (insurance and hospital staff that review the patient's records for continued stay and appropriateness of treatment) will use the improved documentation to substantiate the patient's need for continued treatment.

The Profession

Improved documentation will substantiate the need for care and validate the appropriate level for care.

It is unlikely that the posturing between providers and insurance companies will ever go away. But the perception that mental health interventions lack empirical evidence and that providers keep patients until their insurance runs out will eventually change as mental health providers improve their documentation, substantiate the need for patient care, and demonstrate the desired treatment outcomes.

CHAPTER 3 SELF-TEST

Answer the following questions. When you have completed the test, check your answers in Appendix B.

1. What are two reasons therapists historically give for not completing treatment plans?

2. What are the two reasons Walt Disney believed people failed?

3. CMS requires staff to specify four distinct parts for every intervention on the treatment plan. Name them.

4. What are two benefits of good treatment planning for a facility?

He is wise who knows the source of knowledge . . . .
— **A. A. Hodge**

The *Diagnostic and Statistical Manual of Mental Disorders*

| **4**

The wise man is not one who knows everything, but where to find everything.

THE *DIAGNOSTIC AND STATISTICAL MANUAL OF MENTAL DISORDERS*, FOURTH EDITION, TEXT REVISION

The American Psychiatric Association's *Diagnostic and Statistical Manual of Mental Disorders,* Fourth Edition, Text Revision, or the *DSM-IV-TR*, is *the source* of psychiatric diagnostics for mental health professionals. Effective treatment of any patient depends on an accurate diagnosis, and the *DSM-IV-TR* is the basis for mental health diagnostics.

In order to understand treatment planning, the mental health professional must have a working knowledge of the *DSM-IV-TR*. This chapter provides an overview of its historical development. It also includes some examples of how practitioners use the *DSM-IV-TR* to diagnose behavioral health patients.

The History of the *Diagnostic and Statistical Manual*

There have been five previous editions of the *DSM*. Here is a short description of the different versions.

- *DSM–I (1952)*
  The first edition of the *DSM* appeared in 1952. It placed a very strong emphasis on symptoms being a reaction of the personality to biopsychosocial stressors.
- *DSM–II (1968)*
  This edition matched the ICD-8 (International Classification of Diseases).

  IMPORTANT CONCEPTUAL THEORY

  The terms in the *DSM–II* did not relate to specific theoretical frameworks. Therefore, it was not necessary to understand how different schools or disciplines viewed treatment to use the manual.

- *DSM–III (1980)*
  This was the first edition of the *DSM* to address the multiaxial approach to diagnostic evaluation. This version used diagnostic criteria to clarify and increase the accuracy and dependability of the diagnosis.
- *DSM–III–R (1987)*
  This edition revised and clarified much of the information presented in the *DSM–III*.
- *DSM–IV (1994)*
  The purpose of the *DSM-IV* was to provide clean descriptions of diagnostic categories in order to enable clinicians and investigators to diagnose, communicate about, study, and treat people with various mental disorders. One of the most important features of the *DSM-IV* is its provision of diagnostic criteria to improve the reliability of diagnostic judgments.
- *DSM-IV-TR(2000)*
  This is the current edition of the *Diagnostic and Statistical Manual of Mental Disorders.*

Basic Features of the *DSM-IV-TR*

The *DSM-IV-TR* is a comprehensive listing of psychiatric diagnoses and mental disorders. The classification system for the *DSM-IV-TR* defines clinically significant behavior that is associated with present problems.

IMPORTANT CONCEPTUAL THEORY

It is important to note that the *DSM* does not classify people, but rather the disorders that they have. The *DSM* does not deal with the etiology of mental disorders. In fact, the etiology of most mental illness is unknown. Therefore, the *DSM* simply tries to give a description of the clinical symptomology and does not depend on any theoretical framework or school of therapy. These descriptions of clinical symptomology are *diagnostic criteria*.

Each set of diagnostic criteria, grouped in a certain manner, represents a specific diagnosis. Simplified, this means that a specific combination of biopsychosocial problems defines each diagnosis. The pieces make up the whole. When enough of the corresponding symptoms are present, they verify the correct diagnosis.

Conversely, if the diagnostic criterion does not match the diagnosis, the diagnosis is incorrect.

Multiaxial Diagnosis *DSM–III* was the first edition of the manual to recognize a multiaxial diagnostic format. This format assured the treatment of all types of clinical issues.

CMS requires that the treatment plan address the patient's needs using a multiaxial system. There are five axes in the *DSM-IV-TR* classification system. Here is a brief description of each axis. It is important to note once more that the *DSM-IV-TR* does not classify people, but rather the disorders that they have.

Axis I—Clinical Disorders and Other Conditions that May Be a Focus of Clinical Attention
Axis I addresses all psychiatric disorders and other conditions in the *DSM–IV-TR*. The staff should list multiple Axis I diagnoses, in order of severity. In other words, the principle diagnosis (what brought the patient into treatment) is the first diagnosis on the list.

The staff can choose to defer any diagnosis on all five axes of the multiaxial system. That is, the clinician may recognize that a diagnosis is present but choose not to deal with it at this time. When a patient has diagnoses on Axis I, II, and III, the Axis I diagnosis is primary and considered the reason for treatment. Examples of Axis I diagnoses are:

296.0—Bipolar disorder, single manic episode

291.8—Alcohol withdrawal

296.2—Major depressive disorder, single episode

Each diagnosis is labeled with a four-digit code. Sometimes, it may be necessary to append additional information or specifics that help further clarify the diagnosis. This clarification is done by adding a fifth digit to the diagnsotic code that denotes the current state of the disorder. The fifth-digit codes are:

1 = Mild

2 = Moderate

3 = Severe without psychotic features

4 = Severe with psychotic features

5 = In partial remission

6 = In full remission

0 = Unspecified

V-Codes are conditions not attributable to a mental disorder, but are nonetheless appropriate for professional intervention. Many clinicians refer to these conditions as relational problems. Examples of V-Codes are:

V61.21—Physical abuse of a child

V61.1—Physical abuse of an adult

V65.2—Malingering

V15.81—Noncompliance with treatment

V-Codes are recorded on Axis I.

Axis II—Personality Disorders and Mental Retardation

Axis II focuses on personality disorders and conditions of mental retardation, as well as maladaptive personality features and defense mechanisms. Axis II diagnoses insure that these specific diagnostic issues are considered and that the clinician does not focus solely on Axis I problems. Examples of Axis II diagnoses are:

317—Mild mental retardation

313.51—Expressive language disorder

312.8—Conduct disorder

Axis III—General medical conditions

Axis III must include all pertinent medical diagnoses that exacerbate the mental disorder. Examples are diabetes or high blood pressure. Additionally, any general medical disorder that is severe enough to warrant active care during the current period of treatment needs addressing on Axis III of the treatment plan. It is important to note that surveyors are very particular about Axis III diagnoses. Even though the *DSM–IV–TR* says that clinicians must deal with *only* those problems that relate to the psychiatric condition or are serious enough to merit freestanding treatment, it is imperative that all recognized medical diagnoses be followed to their logical conclusion. In fact, many medical problems create symptomology that mimics psychiatric disorders. The purpose of evaluating Axis III diagnosis is to rule out medical causes of the presenting problems. Here are some examples:

MEDICAL DIAGNOSIS	PSYCHIATRIC SYMPTOMOLOGY
Multiple sclerosis	Depression, mood swings, personality changes
Temporal lobe epilepsy	Delusions, confusion, depression, angry outbursts
Anemia	Guilt, anxiety, depression
Brain tumor	Depression, memory loss, personality change
Wilson's disease	Explosiveness, mood swings, delusions
Congestive heart failure	Delusions

AXIS IV—Psychosocial and Environmental Problems

Axis IV chronicles the patient's psychosocial problems and environment. Unlike the *DSM-III-R*, which asked the clinician to list two problems that precipitated the present hospitalization, the *DSM-IV-TR* asks the clinician to address nine specific areas of concern. These areas are as follows:

1. Problems with the primary support group
2. Problems relating to the social environment
3. Educational problems
4. Occupational problems
5. Housing problems
6. Economic problems
7. Problems with access to health care
8. Problems related to interaction with the legal system
9. Other psychological and environmental problems

The definition and a brief description of these groups of psychosocial stressors are in the *DSM-IV-TR*. It is reproduced here in Figure 4.1.

The diagnostician should be careful to address each area of concern when completing the documentation for this diagnostic area.

AXIS V—Global Assessment of Functioning

Axis V is commonly called the GAF scale. The GAF scale addresses the patient's psychological, social, and occupational functioning. The staff should assess the patient using the GAF scale at least twice during hospitalization. The patient's levels of functioning for the *prior year* and on *admission* will help document the need for care.

The diagnostician must be sure that his or her ratings accurately reflect the patient's level of functioning. Many mental health professionals ignore this scale or rely on their memory to rate their patients. This can lead to inaccurately documenting the patient's level of functioning. *Many times this single action is responsible for insurance companies denying the claim based on lack of medical necessity.*

The definition and description of the suggested form used to document the GAF scale can be found in the *DSM-IV-TR*. It is reproduced here in Figure 4.2.

When the clinician uses all five axes of the *DSM-IV-TR*, it ensures a "holistic" view of the patient.

Diagnosis Status Sheet   An efficient way to keep track of a patient's diagnoses is a Diagnosis Status Sheet. This status sheet should include the following information:

Figure 4.1 | Axis IV Psychosocial Stressors

Axis IV
Psychosocial Stressors

Addressograph Imprint

Problem with Primary Support Group:_____
_____
_____

Death of family member, health problems in family disruption of family by separation; divorce or estrangement; removal from the home; remarriage
of a parent; sexual or physical abuse parental over-protection neglect of a child;- inadequate discipline, discord with siblings; birth of a sibling.

Problem Relating to the Social Environment:_____
_____
_____

Death or loss of a friend, inadequate social support, living alone; difficulty with acculturation discrimination; adjustment to lifestyle transition (such a retirement

Educational Problems:_____
_____
_____

Illiteracy; academic problems-, discord with teachers or classmate inadequate school or environment

Occupational Problems:_____
_____
_____

Unemployment threat of job loss; difficult work schedule, difficult work conditions; job change discord with boss or co-workers.

Housing Problems:_____
_____
_____

hopelessness; inadequate housing; unsafe neighborhood; discord with neighbors or landlord

Economic Problems:_____
_____
_____

Extreme poverty inadequate finances insufficient welfare support

Problems with Access to Health Care Services:_____
_____
_____

inadequate health care services; transportation to health care facilities unavailable, inadequate health care insurance

Problems Related to Interaction with the Legal System/Crime:_____
_____
_____

arrest; incarceration; litigation; victim of crime

Other Psychological and Environmental Problems:_____
_____
_____

Exposure to disease, war, other hostilities; discord with non-family care giver such as counselors, social workers or physicians, unavailability of social agencies

_____

Figure 4.2 | Axis V GAF Scale

	Axis V GAF Scale
Addressograph Imprint	

100-91

- Superior functioning in a wide range of activities, life's problems never seem to get out of hand, is sought out by others because of his or her many positive qualities. No symptoms-

90-81

- Absent or minimal symptoms (e.g., mild anxiety before an exam), good functioning in all areas, interested and involved in a wide range of activities, socially effective, generally satisfied with life, no more than everyday problems or concerns (e.g.., an occasional argument with family members).

80-71

- If symptoms are present, they are transient and expectable reactions to psychosocial stressors (e.g., difficulty concentrating after family y argument) no more than slight impairment in social, occupational, Or school functioning (e.g., temporarily falling behind in schoolwork).

70-61

- Some Mild symptoms (e.g., depressed mood and mild insomnia) OR some difficulty in social, occupational, or school functioning (e.g., occasional truancy, or theft within the household), but generally functioning pretty well, has some meaningful interpersonal relationships

60-51

- Moderate symptoms (e.g., flat effect and circumstantial speech, occasional panic attacks, OR moderate difficulty in social, occupational, or school functioning (e.g., few friends, unable to keep a job).

50-41

- Serious symptoms (e.g., suicidal ideation, severe obsessional rituals, frequent shoplifting) OR any serious impairment in social, occupational, or school functioning, (e.g., no friends, unable to keep a job).

40-31

- Some impairment in reality testing or communication (e.g., speech is at times illogical, obscure, or irrelevant), OR major impairment in several areas, such as work or school, family relations, judgment, thinking or mood (e-g-, depressed man avoids friends, neglects family, and is unable to work, child frequently beats up younger children, is defiant at home, and is failing at school).

30-21

- Behavior is considerably influenced by delusions or hallucinations OR serious impairment In communication or judgment (e.g., sometimes incoherent, acts grossly inappropriately, suicidal preoccupation) OR inability to function in almost all areas (e.g., stays in bed all day, no job, home, friends).

20-11

- Some danger of hurting self or others (e.g., suicide attempts without dear expectation of death, frequently violent; manic excitement OR occasionally fails; to maintain minimal personal hygiene (e.g., smears feces) OR gross impairment in communication (e.g., largely incoherent or mute).

10-1

- Persistent danger of severely hurting self Or Others (recurrent violence) OR persistent inability to maintain minimal Personal hygiene OR serious suicidal act with clears expectation of death.

0

- Inadequate information

GAF Score Prior Year	GAF Score on Admission	GAF Score on Discharge

---

- A list of each diagnosis that was identified during this episode of care (on all five axes).
- The status of each diagnosis.

Shortened length of stays reduce the treatment team's ability to focus on a broad number of diagnoses. But CMS surveyors actively seek all identified diagnoses and check to see if all of them have been treated and come to a logical conclusion about them. Therefore, the team must identify all of the diagnosis present and indicate those that require active management. The staff can use a Diagnosis Status Sheet for this purpose.

Each diagnosis can have one of several treatment status designations. These designations identify how the treatment team is to manage the patient's treatment. Identified diagnoses are placed in one of the following five categories:

1. Active—The diagnosis will be actively pursued during this course of treatment.
2. Refused—The diagnosis has been identified for treatment and the patient has *refused* treatment at this time.
3. Deferred—Some diagnosis will be *deferred*. Although this diagnosis requires care, they do not need to be actively treated during this course of treatment.
4. Maintained—This is an existing diagnosis with an existing plan of care, which we will *maintain*.
5. Completed—This diagnosis is *completed*. The patient has achieved closure and the desired therapeutic results have been achieved.

Once the status of a diagnosis has been determined, the staff documents the diagnosis on the problem list. Please review the Diagnosis Sheet, shown in Figure 4.3.

IMPORTANT NOTE

When using the Diagnosis Sheet, any diagnosis, not otherwise designated, is an active problem.

SUMMARY

The *DSM–IV-TR* lists and identifies criteria used to diagnose physical and mental disorders, and provides documentation of the patient's current level of function in his or her environment. When a patient presents enough of the appropriate diagnostic criteria, the clinician is able to document the appropriate diagnosis, using all five axes.

Furthermore, addressing diagnoses on all five axes ensures that all appropriate biopsychosocial issues are treated.

IMPORTANT NOTE

This chapter is as an introduction and basic overview to the *DSM-IV-TR*. Actual use of the *DSM–IV-TR* is a great deal more complicated. Only qualified, trained mental health professionals should engage in behavioral health diagnostics.

Author and physician James Morrison discusses in his book *DSM-IV Made Easy*, the enormous challenges posed by the *DSM-IV-TR* for any professional person who has worked with it. It was written by a committee and worded to satisfy the demands of researchers, lawyers, and clinicians. The result is that it may please none of them.

Figure 4.3 | Axis I, II & III Diagnosis Sheet

Addressograph Imprint	**Axis I, II & III Diagnosis Sheet**

AXIS I DIAGNOSIS

	C	D	M	R
_____	C	D	M	R
_____	C	D	M	R
_____	C	D	M	R
_____	C	D	M	R
_____	C	D	M	R
_____	C	D	M	R
_____	C	D	M	R
_____	C	D	M	R

AXIS II DIAGNOSIS

	C	D	M	R
_____	C	D	M	R
_____	C	D	M	R
_____	C	D	M	R

AXIS III DIAGNOSIS

	C	D	M	R
_____	C	D	M	R
_____	C	D	M	R
_____	C	D	M	R
_____	C	D	M	R
_____	C	D	M	R
_____	C	D	M	R
_____	C	D	M	R
_____	C	D	M	R

DIAGNOSIS CODES

C	This diagnosis is COMPLETED. The patient has achieved closure and the desired therapeutic results have been achieved
D	This diagnosis is DEFERRED. Although the problem requires care, it does not need to be actively treated at this time
M	This diagnosis is an existing problem with an existing plan of care which we will MAINTAIN
R	This diagnosis has been identified for treatment, however the patient has REFUSED treatment

For this reason, it will be necessary for students to study the *DSM-IV-TR* and learn more about the process of multiaxial diagnostics.

Here are some suggested texts to help students gain further insight into the diagnostic process:

- Morrison, James. (1995). *The DSM-IV-TR Made Easy*. Kitty Moore, ed. New York: Guilford.
- Kaplan, Harold, MD, and Benjamin Sadock, MD. (1998). *Synopsis of Psychiatry: Behavioral Sciences/Clinical Psychiatry*. Philadelphia: Lippincott Williams & Wilkins.

CHAPTER 4 SELF-TEST

Answer the following questions. When you have completed the test, check your answers in Appendix B.

1. What are diagnostic criteria?

2. What is a multiaxial diagnosis and why is it useful in treating mental disorders?

3. What does the fifth digit of a diagnostic code denote?

4. What types of disorders belong on the following axes?
   Axis I

   Axis II

   Axis III

   Axis IV

   Axis V

5. What is a V-Code? On what axis do you record it?

Quick decisions are unsafe decisions . . .
— **Sophocles**

The Diagnosis

An old error is more popular than a new truth.

GETTING IT RIGHT!

So much of successful treatment depends on the right beginning. Once treatment starts down the wrong path, it is difficult to change the momentum. In mental health settings, treatment begins with a diagnosis. As we discussed in the last chapter, constructing the correct diagnosis is a matter of validating diagnostic criteria with the standards in the *DSM-IV-TR* for that particular diagnosis.

Getting the right diagnosis is much simpler in theory than it is in practice. Confirming the right diagnosis for treatment is a process that usually develops during the first few office visits either as an outpatient or in the hospital. Here is an overview of that process.

CMS STANDARDS

Portions of this text originate from the CMS Clinical Records Standards. When you see the ⌁ icon, it will be followed by the appropriate CMS standard or tag number. These passages are reproduced exactly as they appear in the CMS standards. The author and publisher have not edited the grammar or spelling. A full copy of the clinical standards text can be found in Appendix A at the back of this workbook.

Admission

The entire admission or "front end" process of any behavioral health setting prepares the team to effectively deal with the patient and the problems that lead him or her to seek help. The entire combination of these problems or symptoms equals the diagnosis.

The first step of any treatment process is deciding on a diagnosis. There are many forms of diagnosis. Here are definitions for the three different types of diagnoses generally used in treatment:

- Admission Diagnosis—When a patient is admitted to most behavioral health treatment settings, he or she is required to have a diagnosis. The admission diagnosis is usually derived from a brief intake assessment and clinical history. Because the intake assessment is usually an abbreviated process, the admission diagnosis may not be the final diagnosis used to develop the treatment plan. Rather, it is a beginning point in treatment. The treatment team will "firm up" the diagnosis as more clinical information becomes available.

- Rule-Out or Provisional Diagnosis—The *DSM-IV-TR* says, the *provisional* specifier can be used when the clinician expects that the full criteria for the diagnosis will ultimately be met and there is inadequate information available for a firm diagnosis at the present time. When a diagnostician suspects that the patient has a certain diagnosis, but wants to rule out other etiologies or causes before giving a substantiated diagnosis, a rule-out diagnosis is used. Physicians and other allied health professionals with admission privileges often use rule-out or provisional diagnoses when they admit a patient and have not seen the patient.

- Substantiated Diagnosis—"The substantiated diagnosis serves as the basis for treatment interventions. A substantiated diagnosis is the diagnosis identified by the treatment team to be the primary focus upon which treatment planning will be based. It evolves from the synthesis of data from the various disciplines." ☞ B120   When the master treatment plan is opened 72 hours after admission (in an inpatient setting), the diagnosis must be substantiated.

Let us begin by examining how each type of diagnosis develops.

The Admission Diagnosis

If a treatment plan is going to get off kilter, it usually starts during admission. Every day, thousands of patients seek help from mental health professionals. In a hospital setting, the patient shows up in emergency rooms or admissions departments for evaluation and assessment. Very few hospitals or other treatment settings use physicians to do admission assessments. Trained mental health professionals are typically responsible for gathering the patient's information. After they complete the initial intake screening, the intake specialist relays the information to an on-call or consulting physician. At this point, the physician, or in some cases another credentialed mental health professional, either gives permission to admit the patient or instructions for the continued disposition of the case.

ADMISSION PRIVILEGES

Some mental health professionals are credentialed to admit patients to hospitals and other treatment environments. In these cases the hospital policy dictates that a mental health professional, such as a psychologist or MFCC (Marriage, Family, Child Counselor), has presented credentials that qualifies him or her for admission privileges at the facility. In these specific cases, where appropriate, the term *credentialed mental health professional* can be substituted for the term *physician*.

Many variables will determine whether the patient is seen by a physician prior to admission. These issues may include hospital protocol, the time or circumstances of the admission, the physician referral source relationship, and the client history. If the physician chooses to admit the patient, he or she cannot do so without giving an admission diagnosis. Because the physician is working on secondhand information, he or she uses a rule-out or provisional diagnosis. Most treatment environments do not insist that the physician see a patient face-to-face before admission, therefore this is how the system compensates.

The Rule-Out or Provisional Diagnosis

CMS recognizes the problems inherent in admission systems, and is cognizant of the fact that physicians are not omnipotent. Therefore, they allow physicians to give rule-out and/or provisional diagnosis for up to 72 hours while the treatment team gathers more information about the patient. CMS clearly states that "[r]ule-out diagnoses, by themselves are not acceptable as a substantiated diagnosis." ☞ B120 Within 72 hours, and before the team opens the master treatment plan, they must substantiate the diagnosis.

The problem is that the first diagnostic impression, right or wrong, is often what remains on the treatment plan. It is easier to continue down the wrong path than to change the initial course of thinking. In fact, many patients leave the hospital with their initial diagnosis intact. Days later, when the discharge note is dictated, the treating physician will record a different, final diagnosis.

If the patient does not receive a substantiated diagnosis before treatment begins, there is an excellent chance that the patient will receive inappropriate care and the plan for treatment will be ineffective.

Substantiated Diagnosis

In order to begin effective treatment, the treatment team must agree that the patient is exhibiting symptoms that correlate to the criteria, V-Codes, and associated features in the *DSM-IV-TR* that match their diagnosis. Otherwise, the treatment team would begin by treating the wrong set of problems.

Notice that the specific task of gathering information to make a substantiated diagnosis is *not* the physician's alone. CMS expects the patient will receive treatment from a variety of treatment specialists. This is an interdisciplinary or multidisciplinary team style of treatment. Each discipline on the team is responsible for evaluating the patient from their particular field of expertise. After their assessments are complete, each discipline will decide how to apply their specific training to create interventions that help the patient. The number and types of disciplines represented on the treatment team will vary, based on the types of problems to be treated. At a minimum, a treatment team will always have a physician and a nurse.

The structure is clear; all participating disciplines must help substantiate the patient's diagnosis and participate in designing a plan for recovery.

Substantiating a Diagnosis   When a physician makes a diagnosis, he or she begins by saying, "The last time I saw this set of symptoms, the patient had this diagnosis." This is essentially how the rule-out or provisional diagnosis happens. If a patient came to a physician's office complaining of a 103° fever with white pustules in the throat, malaise, difficulty swallowing, and general body aches, the physician would probably begin by ruling out a diagnosis of strep throat. In order to be certain the diagnosis was correct, the physician would rely on other trained professionals, such as the lab technician, to do additional tests. Doing a culture and sensitivity (a laboratory procedure that uses a cotton swab to gather material from a patient's throat in order to grow a culture to correctly identify the infecting organism) and a white blood cell count would complete the clinical picture and form the basis for an accurate, substantiated diagnosis.

The physician could begin treatment without these tests, but the original diagnosis would still just be a guess. The additional lab information ensures successful treatment.

In mental health treatment, clinicians also gather additional information as necessary to substantiate a diagnosis. This process begins with a variety of discipline-specific assessments. Different assessment tools help the team obtain a holistic picture of the patient's needs.

Now that we have the patient's admission (preliminary) diagnosis, let us move on and review some different types of assessments the team uses to substantiate that diagnosis.

CHAPTER 5 SELF-TEST

Answer the following questions. When you have completed the test, check your answers in Appendix B.

1. What are the two main objectives of mental health assessments?

2. How long does CMS allow the treatment team to use a provisional or rule-out diagnosis?

3. Define the following terms:

   Admission diagnosis

   Provisional diagnosis

   Rule-out diagnosis

   Substantiated diagnosis

4. What does the term *multidisciplinary treatment team* mean?

5. What is the minimum number of treatment team members and what disciplines must they represent?

For a generation of therapists, who have never known anything else, thinking of their therapeutic role as a technician rather than an artist may not be that troubling. — **Jeffrey A. Katter**

Assessments

LET'S GET STARTED!

As we discovered in the last chapter, so much of successful treatment depends on the right beginning. Once the admitting physician or treating professional gives the team a diagnosis to work with, the team must either substantiate or disprove that diagnosis based on the clinical information gathered in their assessments.

Although there are many types of assessments, they all serve essentially the same two purposes: (a) substantiating the diagnosis, and (b) discovering what patient strengths the team intends to draw upon to help the patient gain insight into his or her problems. This insight and a commitment to continued therapy will prepare the patient to move along the continuum of care.

Treatment planning information comes from a required "inventory of the patient's assets." ➯ B117 This standard defines what is and is not to be considered a patient asset. Generally, the terms "strength" and "asset" are interchangeable. However, for the purpose of treatment planning, not all strengths are relevant or useful. Strengths are personal attributes like knowledge, interests, skills, aptitudes, employment status, and environmental resources (family) that may be useful in developing a meaningful treatment plan. For instance, a patient who has the ability to verbalize feelings would be a good candidate for emotive types of therapies. If a patient is intelligent or well educated, cognitive types of therapy would seem to be an appropriate approach. The real issue is to identify the patient's strengths and devise ways that the patient can use them to assist in the therapeutic process.

CMS gives further clarification on the standard: "For the purpose of the regulation, words such as 'Youth,' 'Pretty,' 'Social Security Income,' and 'has a car' do not represent assets." ➯ B117

The team also has to sort out the problems or "disabilities" which precipitated the patient seeking treatment, and decide which of the problems needs fixing and in what order.

CMS uses the terms "disability" and "problem" interchangeably. CMS standards essentially say that any biopsychosocial problem needing remedy must be considered for treatment during the assessments. (See Section B119.) Obviously, the term biopsychosocial refers to biological, psychological, and social problems.

It may be helpful to think of problems in the following terms:

- Biological = Medical or physiological problems
- Psychological = Problems with personality, feelings, thoughts, or intellect
- Sociological = Environmental and social problems that include family, social, and institutional relationships

Now, the team has a good idea of the types of issues the patient must deal with in treatment. They also have a good overview of their patient's capacity to handle those problems. Using this knowledge, they can begin a battery of discipline-specific assessments that will create a well-rounded evaluation for substantiating the original diagnosis.

Who Must Do Evaluations?

In most settings, CMS is not specific about what disciplines must be represented on a treatment team. In fact, the number of team members is directly proportional to how long the patient will stay in treatment (length of stay). "The briefer the hospital stay, the fewer disciplines may be involved in the patient's treatment." ☞ B119

Here is the usual range of assessments done in an inpatient treatment setting.

- History and Physical (H&P) (within the first 24 hours)—"Upon admission the patient should receive a thorough history and physical examination with all indicated laboratory examinations." ☞ B109 Most psychiatrists consider the invasive types of body contact necessary for a good H&P to be counterproductive to subsequent therapy. Therefore the H&P is usually completed by another physician with a specialty in physical medicine (for example, family practice or internal medicine). The H&P is used to get a concrete measurement of what physical problems exist and how they either exacerbate the psychiatric problems or require separate treatment because of their severity. Components of the H&P include:

    1. An investigation "to discover all structural, functional, systemic and metabolic disorders." ☞ B109
    2. "A thorough history of the patient's past physical disorders, head trauma, accidents, substance dependence/abuse, exposure to toxic agents, tumors, infections, seizures, or temporary loss of consciousness and headaches." ☞ B109
    3. "[s]igns of any current illness since psychotic symptoms may be due to a general medical condition or substance related disorder." ☞ B109
    4. "The physician will perform a 'screening' neurological examination . . . to assess gross function of the various divisions of the central nervous system." ☞ B109

    At a minimum, the H&P will include enough information to assess the patient's physical problems and decide how to handle the medical problems listed on Axis III.

- Psychiatric Evaluation—The psychiatric evaluation must "be completed within 60 hours of admission." ☞ B111 The team psychiatrist provides this clinical assessment to determine the appropriate diagnosis and treatment; therefore, it must contain enough information to "justify the diagnosis and treatment." ☞ B110

    CMS requirements state that the psychiatric evaluation should include the following:

1. The patient's chief complaint.
2. Past history of psychiatric problems or treatment.
3. Past family, educational, vocational, occupational, and social history.
4. Signs of the specific symptoms and diagnostic criteria necessary to justify the diagnosis.
5. A "non-psychiatric medical history including physical disabilities, mental retardation and treatment." ▱ B112
6. "Contain a record of mental status" ▱ B113 including appearance, behavior, emotional responses, verbalization, thought content, and cognition of the patient and observed by the examiner at the time of examination. The mental status exam that is part of the psychiatric evaluation (psych-eval) is a relatively complex process. The treatment staff or professional will use components of the mental status exam on an almost daily basis to review the patient's level of functioning and other issues such as orientation to time, place, or date. From this information, the staff can conclude the level of patient functioning. It is not acceptable to document that the patient is "oriented, memory intact, judgment poor and insight nil," without any supportive information.
7. Notation of "the onset of illness and the circumstances leading to admission." ▱ B114
8. Description of "behavior(s) which require change in order for the patient to function in a less restrictive setting. The identified problems may also include behavioral or relationship difficulties with significant others which require active treatment in order to facilitate a successful discharge." ▱ B115
9. "Estimate intellectual functioning, memory functioning and orientation." ▱ B116
10. "Include an inventory of the patient's assets in descriptive, not interpretive fashion." ▱ B117

Upon completion of this assessment, the treatment team should at least have the diagnoses for Axis I, II, IV, and V of the treatment plan.

• Psychosocial Evaluation (completed within 72 hours)—This clinical evaluation is done by the social worker. The CMS standard states, "the social service records, including reports of interviews with the patients, family members, and others, must provide and assessment of home plans and family attitudes, and community resource contacts as well as a social history." ▱ 108

All patients must have a psychosocial history/assessment. It *must* address the following three components:

1. Factual and historical information
2. Social evaluation
3. Conclusions and recommendations

A good psychosocial evaluation should also include a history of past and present relationships, as well as blockages to functioning in the patient's "normal" setting. This assessment of the patient's functional blockages, and the social worker's clinical recommendations for helping the patient cope with them, are the beginnings of a treatment plan.

• Nursing Assessment (completed within 8 hours)—A registered nurse (RN) is responsible for this assessment. The nursing assessment is usually this first to be completed, and will serve as the basis for the immediate implementation of treatment and interventions necessary to protect the patient.

By definition, a facility must provide nursing and medical interventions 24 hours a day, 7 days a week to be considered a hospital. The responsibility for immediate treatment of physical and mental problems begins with a registered nurse and the nursing team. As treatment stays have grown shorter, the emphasis on beginning active treatment at admission has become crucial. Nursing service personnel are critical to successful inpatient psychiatric treatment. The nursing staff is the only discipline that deals with the patient 24 hours a day.

The nursing staff is responsible for assessing and treating psychiatric and nonpsychiatric medical issues; administering medications, education, medical treatments, and lab tests; and monitoring patient safety issues. The nursing evaluation will evaluate the patient's needs and assign a "nursing diagnosis" to all problems. It is *extremely important* to note that a nursing diagnosis *cannot be used* as problem statement.

Problem statements must "identify and precisely describe problem behaviors rather than generalized statements . . . i.e., "alteration in thought process," "ineffective coping," "alteration in mood." ☞ B120

Nursing personnel must be eclectic in their abilities and participate fully in almost all aspects and therapies used in treatment. Additionally, nursing personnel are responsible for the initiation of active treatment for the patient. Often, an initial treatment plan will be created to outline the nursing interventions necessary to initiate and document active treatment until the master treatment plan is opened.

- Leisure Skills Evaluation (completed within 72 hours)—This assessment is usually done by a registered occupational therapist (OT-R), certified occupational therapy assistant (COTA), or recreational therapist (RT). The purpose of this assessment is to determine the patient's level of functioning as it is related to living skills, leisure activities, stress management, occupational skill and training, and physical capabilities for functioning in his or her environment. These therapists' treatment responsibilities range from the patient's physical rehabilitation to planning long-term activities for management of his or her living environment.

- Dietary Assessment (completed within 72 hours)—The Registered Dietitian's (RD) assessment will address many aspects of the patient's well-being. This assessment will tell the treatment team the nutritional status of the patient, as well as other problems that may occur because of dietary needs. The RD, in conjunction with the physician, coordinates and watches for food and drug interactions, and educates the patient and his or her family or caretaker about nutrition and diet.

- Psychological Assessment (completed within 72 hours)—The staff psychologist evaluates the patient in terms of cognitive ability, emotional status, neuropsychological functioning, and personality. This evaluation is essential for writing a treatment plan that the patient can cognitively grasp. After all, why would the team bother to write a treatment plan that the patient cannot understand? The psychologist is also a skilled psychotherapist who may participate in almost all of the treatment modalities, particularly behavioral and relationship issues.

These clinical disciplines and assessments represent the usual composition of a treatment team. After the assessments are completed, the individual disciplines get together in a treatment team meeting to discuss and coordinate their findings. As a team, these highly trained professionals, under the direction of the team psychiatrist, will decide on a substantiated diagnosis, and then sort out what problems to address in the course of treatment.

CHAPTER 6 SELF-TEST

Answer the following questions. When you have completed the test, check your answers in Appendix B.

1. What are the two main objectives of assessments?

2. What is another interchangeable term for a patient's assets?

3. Define the term *biopsychosocial*.

4. How many disciplines must be represented on the treatment team?

5. List the seven major assessments, the disciplines responsible for providing them, and the time frame to complete the assessments.

*There is no problem of human nature which is
insoluble . . .* — **Ralph J. Bunche**

Problems

7

Defining and refining a problem statement is the most difficult task in good
treatment planning.

WHAT IS A PROBLEM?

"A [behavioral] disability is any psychiatric, biopsychosocial problem
requiring treatment intervention." ☞ B119

Earlier we were established that the terms *disability* and *problem* are
interchangeable, thereby defining what a problem is. If only defining
problem statements were this simple in actual treatment planning, the task
would be much easier.

Individuals presenting themselves for treatment have many problems; the
treatment team must weed out the issues that do not have a bearing on the
treatment episode at hand (see Figure 7.1).

Only those problems that keep a patient in the current level of the
continuum need addressing in that environment.

Johnson's Rule

The reader should make special note of the following rule as it sets forth an
important conceptual point.

> **JOHNSON'S RULE**
>
> A diagnosis can *never* be a problem statement, unless it is on Axis III, in
> which case it is *always* a problem statement.

A diagnosis, except on Axis III, is too vague to be a problem statement.
CMS states that, "the treatment plan must identify and precisely describe
problem behaviors rather than generalized statements, i.e., 'paranoid,'
'aggressive,' 'depressed,' or generic terminology, i.e., 'alteration in thought
process,' 'ineffective coping,' 'alteration in mood.'" ☞ B120

Look at it like this. If a patient told you that he or she was suffering
from an "alteration in mood," would you have a clue about what was wrong

with the patient? How about if a patient told you that he or she was suffering from a "depressed mood." Where would you start?

You would start by reducing the generalized statements into problem *behaviors*. In other words, which of the patient's behaviors characterize his or her depressed moods?

Depressed mood can be one of many specific behaviors. Some of the behavioral characteristics or symptoms of depression might be feelings of helplessness, hopelessness, apathy, social isolation, or withdrawal. These are behaviors that we can see, feel, and hear. They are measurable, objective, and behavioral. They are good problem statements.

On Axis III, any diagnosis automatically becomes the problem statement, even though the diagnosis can be broken down into specific symptoms. CMS standard B120 states that the team must be sure to include all physical problems when they require active treatment and if the medical problem interferes with the patient's psychiatric treatment during his or her hospitalization.

Changing Diagnostic Criteria into Problem Statements

Diagnostic criteria substantiate diagnoses. Diagnostic criteria that are broken down into problem statements further substantiate treatment. Conversely, if the treatment team cannot find any problems related to the diagnostic criteria for the patient's diagnosis, chances are the diagnosis is incorrect or needs further refining.

When a patient presents himself or herself for treatment, the staff begins a process of refinement and elimination that will eventually contribute to a substantiated diagnosis.

The accurate identification of these problems and their relationship to the diagnosis is the first step in the treatment progression.

In order to further understand this process, let us take the diagnosis of Major Depressive Disorder and see how the treatment team could convert some of its diagnostic criteria into problem statements.

MAJOR DEPRESSIVE EPISODE

1. *Depressed mood most of the day, nearly every day, as indicated by either subjective report (e.g., feels sad or empty) or observation made by others (e.g., appears tearful).* **Note:** *In children and adolescents, can be irritable mood.*

Just reading the diagnostic criteria gives the team or therapist a great idea of what problem statements to use in the development of a treatment plan. Sadness, tearfulness, or irritability are three behavioral manifestations of this criterion. Some others would be feelings of helplessness, hopelessness, worthlessness, and social withdrawal. These problems further refine the criterion "depressed mood" into measurable problem behaviors.

EXPLANATION: ASSOCIATED FEATURES

The criteria listed after the "Note:" are associated features. They are other manifestations of how the criteria might show up behaviorally for a specific population or group of patients.

2. *Markedly diminished interest or pleasure in all, or almost all, activities most of the day, nearly every day (as indicated by either subjective account or observation made by others).*

Again, the team must consider what behaviors point toward a loss of interest in activities the patient previously enjoyed. Apathy, social isolation

Figure 7.1 | Problem Development Flow Chart

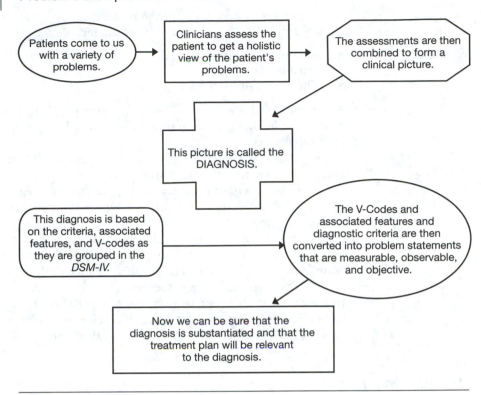

and withdrawal are good examples of behavioral expressions of these criteria. Again, these problem behaviors are measurable and observable.

Let us look at a little different type of criteria:

> 3. *Significant weight loss when not dieting or weight gain (e.g., a change of more than 5% of body weight in a month) or increase or decrease in appetite every day.* **Note:** *In children, consider failure to make expected weight gains.*

Weight loss and weight gain are already measurably defined problem statements. You *can* measure how much weight the patient loses or gains. Therefore, the problem is observable, and measurable, and the problem statement above is a good one.

Let us look at one more scenario. Some criteria could probably stand on their own as problem statements; however, with a little more description, they could change the direction of treatment.

> 4. *Insomnia or hypersomnia nearly every day.*

Insomnia and hypersomnia are straightforward terms. Either the patient is sleeping too much or not enough; both can be good stand-alone problem statements. The twist comes in how these problems present themselves in the particular patient's behavior.

Early morning awakening is one form of insomnia; night terrors and an inability to go to sleep are others. Although they are all forms of insomnia, each behavior would require very different interventions.

The treatment team must be very careful to describe each problem statement as accurately as possible in order to ensure correct management of the situation.

The Problem List

Treatment teams keep track of the problems they have chosen to treat using a "problem list." This problem list should include the following information:

- A numerical listing of each problem identified and treated during this episode of care.
- The status of each problem.

A specific "problem number" identifies each problem. If a patient had three problems identified for treatment, they would be numbered 1 through 3 on the problem list.

By numbering problems, the treatment team can identify and relate other pieces of information and charting documentation to a specific problem. Additionally, there are several other different designations assigned to problems. These designations tell us how the team or therapist has chosen to manage the problem.

As we have discussed, not all problems receive active treatment during a patient's hospitalization. It is the responsibility of the treatment team to deal with "active" problems; that is, problems related to the present need for care.

However, because only the active problems identified are to receive treatment in the current treatment setting, the therapist or treatment team must document that they recognize the presence of other problems and show that they have chosen not to treat them at this time.

Problem Status

Shortened lengths of stay also reduce the treatment team's ability to focus on a broad number of active problems. CMS surveyors look only for these problems that have been identified and treated. Therefore, the treatment team must identify all of the problems they want to actively deal with and acknowledge the existence of other problems. These problems are given a nonactive status. This process is recorded on the problem list.

Identified problems are placed in one of the following five categories:

1. *Active*—A problem that will be actively pursued during this course of treatment.
2. *Refused*—A problem that has been identified for treatment; however, the patient has refused treatment at this time.
3. *Deferred*—A problem that requires care, but does not need to be actively treated during this course of treatment.
4. *Maintained*—An existing problem with an existing plan of care that the treatment team will maintain during this course of treatment.
5. *Completed*—A problem is completed when the patient has achieved closure and the desired therapeutic results have been achieved.

Once the status of a problem has been determined, it is added to the problem list (Figure 7.2 is an example of such a form). All problems not otherwise designated are active problems. Notice that medical and psychiatric/psychological problems are listed separately. Surveyors historically will follow all medical problems to their logical conclusions. If you recognize a medical problem, be sure to designate how you intend to deal with or defer the problem before you move on.

Now that the team has selected the initial problems, they can document the progress toward resolving them. The problem resolution plan is the form used to document the plan of care. At the end of this chapter we will translate our "sample problem" into a suggested format.

Figure 7.2 | Master Treatment Plan Problem List

	Master Treatment Plan Problem List
Addressograph Imprint	

AXIS I&II (Psychiatric, Psychological and Problems with Mental Retardation

Date Opened	Problem #	Problem Description	Problem Status	Date Changed
___/___/___	_____	_____	C D M R	___/___/___
___/___/___	_____	_____	C D M R	___/___/___
___/___/___	_____	_____	C D M R	___/___/___
___/___/___	_____	_____	C D M R	___/___/___
___/___/___	_____	_____	C D M R	___/___/___
___/___/___	_____	_____	C D M R	___/___/___
___/___/___	_____	_____	C D M R	___/___/___
___/___/___	_____	_____	C D M R	___/___/___

AXIS III (Medical Problems)*

*Remember all Axis III diagnosis must be opened as problem statements

Date Changed

Date Opened	Problem #	Problem Description	Problem Status	Date Changed
___/___/___	_____	_____	C D M R	___/___/___
___/___/___	_____	_____	C D M R	___/___/___
___/___/___	_____	_____	C D M R	___/___/___
___/___/___	_____	_____	C D M R	___/___/___
___/___/___	_____	_____	C D M R	___/___/___
___/___/___	_____	_____	C D M R	___/___/___
___/___/___	_____	_____	C D M R	___/___/___
___/___/___	_____	_____	C D M R	___/___/___
___/___/___	_____	_____	C D M R	___/___/___

PROBLEM CODES

C	This problem is COMPLETED. The patient has achieved closure and the desired therapeutic results have been achieved
D	This problem is DEFERRED. although the problem requires care, it does not need to be actively treated at this time
M	This problem is an existing problem with an existing plan of care which we will MAINTAIN
R	This problem has been identified for treatment, however the patient has REFUSED treatment

Manifestations

Now that the team has decided which problem requires active treatment, the next step is to list the behavioral manifestations of that disability. The treatment team must describe and document how that problem manifests itself in a particular patient. In other words, the team should ask, "What does this behavior look like in our patient?"

Manifestations vary by patient and treatment environment. The treatment team must take care to describe what is going on with their patient. Be specific when you describe what is going on with your patient and use enough detail so that any team member reading the manifestation can easily identify the behavior to be treated. You may know what you're dealing with, but you are not there to tell other staff what to look for 24 hours a day.

Remember, problem clarity is the key to problem resolution.

Let us examine a couple of different ways the problem of "social isolation" might manifest as behaviors.

> Ms. Jones refuses to leave her house. She stays inside, and does not respond to knocking at her door or telephone calls. She has been doing this for two weeks.

Or:

> Ms. Jones has locked herself inside her darkened bedroom for two days. She curls up in the corner of her room and pulls a blanket over her head.

Or, consider this manifestation for an outpatient setting:

> Ms. Jones has no desire to participate in her usual weekly activities. She does not want to play bridge with her friends and refuses to go out unless it is absolutely necessary.

Each of these manifestations describes a form of social isolation, but each is a very different state of affairs. Ms. Jones locking herself in a dark room, curling up with a blanket, and refusing to come out, is a much more serious problem than her not wanting to go to her bridge club. This additional information and detail will lead to different treatment interventions, expectations, settings, and outcomes.

In summary, the team has:

1. Substantiated the diagnosis.
2. Broken it into manageable problem statements.
3. Defined how that problem shows up in their patient's behavior.

Figure 7.3 presents a suggested format for documenting this information.

Figure 7.3 | Problem Resolution Plan

	Problem Resolution Plan	Jones, Mrs. Ida Lee DOB 11/07/1918 Religious Preference: Catholic Marital Status: Married Admit Date: 8/7/2000 Attending Physician: Dr. Landman
		Addressograph Imprint

PROBLEM #	PROBLEM STATEMENT	DATE OPENED
1	Social Isolation	8/14/2000

MANIFESTATIONS OF THE PROBLEM
What behaviors describes the problem?

Mrs. Jones locks herself inside her darkened bedroom for two days. She curls up in the corner of her room and pulls a blanket over her head.

After the problem name has been transcribed, the manifestation is added to the Problem Resolution Plan

How can the patient dem[onstrate]...[d]ischarged?

LTG #		TARGET DATE

SHORT TERM GOAL
What intermediate step will be used to measure progress toward discharge goal?

STG #		TARGET DATE

#	INTERVENTIONS

List who is responsible for this intervention by name and discipline	List the modality, milieu or treatment group used to do the intervention	Describe the focus of the intervention and the expected result of participation	List the frequency of the intervention

CHAPTER 7 SELF-TEST

Answer the following questions. When you have completed the test, check your answers in Appendix B.

1. What is a problem statement?

2. What is Johnson's rule?

3. Can a nursing diagnosis be used as a problem statement? Explain your answer.

4. What is the difference between a diagnosis, a psychiatric criterion, and a problem statement?

5. What does it mean when a treatment team cannot find problems related to the diagnostic criteria?

6. List three problem statements related to the diagnostic criteria of depressed mood.

7. What is a manifestation and how does it make a difference in the patient's treatment regimen?

8. What is the key to problem resolution?

*If you don't know where you're going, you'll end up
somewhere else . . .* — **Yogi Berra**

Our aspirations are our possibilities. — **Robert Browning**

Long-Term and Short-Term Goals | 8

TREATMENT GOALS

Treatment goals are concrete means of measuring the success of the chosen treatment modalities and interventions. There are many definitions of long-term and short-term goals. This chapter will seek to clarify a system of writing achievable goals in a way that has the greatest relevance to treatment success.

CMS says: "Whether the use of short-term, or a combination of short-term and long-term goals is appropriate is dependent on the length of hospital stay." ☞ 121 The treatment facility or mental health professional needs to decide what type of treatment services are provided. "In crisis intervention and short-term treatment there may be only one time frame for treatment goals. As the length of the hospital stay increases (often because of the long-term chronic nature of the patient's illness), both long range and short term goals are needed." ☞ 121

Here is a checklist for writing successful goals:

✓ The patient and the team/therapist should decide on the patient's goals for treatment.
✓ Make sure that the goals relate to the problem the team is treating.
✓ Write the goals so that they are realistic and achievable for the patient.
✓ All goals must be measurable. That is, the patient must exhibit some observable change in behavior as an outcome for treatment.
✓ All goals must have a time frame. They must include a documented, specific, expected date for achievement.
✓ Both long-term and short-term goals will be written to describe what the patient will accomplish.

Long-Term Goals (LTG)

The terms long-range and long-term goals are synonymous. "Long-term goals are achieved through the development of a series of short-term goals." ☞ B121

In an outpatient setting, long-term goals usually have outcome expectations that will take months or even years to achieve. The same is true of many other nonhospital-based treatment environments. In these settings, the therapist usually plans for a long-term course of treatment. However, managed care is changing the way providers deliver care. The biggest change, for all levels of care, is rapid treatment turnover. Patients just do not stay in any level of care for very long. Although the average length of stay for inpatient settings may vary, most facilities keep psychiatric patients from 3 to 15 days.

Outpatient services vary by insurance policy. The American Psychiatric Association states that patients with severe and persistent mental disorders may need psychotherapy to deal with fluctuating clinical states over many years and as an adjunct in combination with medications.

Although many patients may need years of extended therapy, most insurance policies break treatment into episodes of care based on the current treatment environment. Many insurance companies begin by approving payment for a specific number of outpatient therapy sessions and then approve additional sessions if they become necessary.

Given these parameters, long-range goals should be based on the amount of time the therapist thinks it will take to move the patient out of his or her particular portion of the continuum of care.

If the patient accomplishes a goal after leaving your care, it would be impossible to measure that progress. After all, the patient is gone; you cannot observe him or her! All patient goals require a target date for accomplishment. The treatment team must weigh how long the insurance company will pay for care against the progress the patient can realistically make in that length of stay. Insurance providers will argue that they are not telling the therapist or treatment team how long they can treat patients; rather, they simply manage the patient's insurance policy as contracted.

In order for the therapist or treatment team to create a realistic plan of care, the following definition of long-term goals should be considered.

LONG-TERM GOALS

Long-term goals are measurable, objective indicators that show that the patient/client, family, or caregiver has acquired enough skills/tools to be ready/safe for discharge from the current level of care.

Although long-term goals may be planned for the postdischarge period, treatment in all settings should limit long-term goals to a point in treatment where the therapist/team feels good about discharging the patient and moving him or her to the next level of the continuum of care.

Long-term goals need to be realistic. Not every patient has the same capabilities, and not all treatment outcomes will be identical. Long-term goals should be "stepped" or progressively based on the patient's potential for progress. In some severe cases, the patient will even have to rely on others to help him or her function in the next level of care.

Long-Term Goal Progression

Long-term goals should have one of four different outcome expectations:

1. The best outcome measurement for a long-term goal is complete remission of the problem. The patient and therapist/staff have completely resolved the problem.

2. Sometimes the therapist/team can only improve the patient's level of functioning or reduce the frequency of occurrence of the problem.

3. At times, the best-case scenario is that the patient will have insight into his or her problems and learn to deal with the problems within his or her capabilities to cope.

4. The worst-case scenario is that the patient will need a family member, caretaker, or even another level of care to help resolve the problem over a long period of time. Sometimes a patient will not have the capacity to ever solve the problem.

The treatment team must decide what the patient is realistically able to accomplish prior to discharge.

Using the previously listed guidelines, let us look at some examples of step-down, long-term goals.

Problem Statement: Social Isolation

MANIFESTATION:

Ms. Jones locked herself inside a darkened bedroom for two days. She curls up in the corner of her room and pulls a blanket over her head.

Here are some examples of possible long-term goals:

REMISSION OF THE PROBLEM:

Ms. Jones will verbalize that she no longer needs to be socially isolated and wants to return to her "normal activities."

IMPROVED LEVEL OF FUNCTIONING:

Ms. Jones will not isolate from other patients and staff while she is in the hospital.

Or:

Ms. Jones will increase her social interaction from one hour per day to four hours per day as demonstrated by her staying out of her room.

GAINED INSIGHT AND LIMITED RESPONSE:

Ms. Jones will be able to explain how her depression "triggers" her social isolation and affects her relationships.

NEED FOR CONTINUED CARE:

Ms. Jones will commit to follow-up care with James Smith, MD, and arrange for an appointment before discharge.

All of these long-term goals are perfectly acceptable; the key is to choose the goal that is within the patient's capabilities. The therapist or treatment team and the patient must collaboratively choose the appropriate goal based on the patient's ability to achieve that target in the current treatment setting before discharge.

Short-Term Goals (STG)

Here is a universal definition for short-term goals.

SHORT-TERM GOALS

Short-term goals define and measure the intermediate steps the patient must make to achieve the treatment plan goal for discharge.

In longer-term therapy, short-term goals measure the progress the patient makes toward achieving his or her long-term goals. They define and measure the immediate steps the patient must make toward achieving the treatment plan goal for discharge.

The purpose of short-term goals is to provide:

1. A concrete measurement of the success or failure of treatment intervention.
2. A time frame for treatment interventions. CMS requires that all goals are time limited; dating goals places a time expectation on completion of treatment.
3. Quick, achievable objectives build the patient's confidence in his or her ability to succeed in therapy. Success increases the patient's self-belief that the treatment team can help him or her get better.

Here are some examples of short-term goals added to our sample plan:

Problem Statement: Social Isolation

MANIFESTATION:

Ms. Jones locked herself inside a darkened bedroom for two days. She curls up in the corner of her room and pulls a blanket over her head.

LONG-TERM GOAL:

Ms. Jones will be able to explain how her depression triggers her social isolation and affects her relationships.

Here are examples of possible short-term goals:

SHORT-TERM GOAL:

Ms. Jones will identify and list three reasons she feels the need to isolate herself.

Or:

Ms. Jones will be able to verbalize the correlation between depression and social isolation.

Both of these short-term goals provide the patient with insight into his or her behavior and provide actual exercises to increase insight.

Although the patient will not gain immediate insight (LTG), the treatment team hopes that these exercises will help the patient piece the puzzle together. If not, the therapist/treatment team will need to change the plan.

Many treatment planning texts reflexively support using multiple short-term goals. For the purpose of short-term treatment, one long-term and one short-term goal is usually sufficient. Often, the use of multiple goals becomes confusing.

Problem statements, manifestations, long-term and short-term goals and interventions (discussed in Chapter 9) are recorded on the problem resolution plan. For an example of our hypothetical plan to date, see Figure 8.1.

Figure 8.1 | Problem Resolution Plan

Problem Resolution Plan

Jones, Mrs. Ida Lee
DOB 11/07/1918
Religious Preference: Catholic
Marital Status: Married
Admit Date: 8/7/2000
Attending Physician: Dr. Landman

Addressograph Imprint

PROBLEM #	PROBLEM STATEMENT	DATE OPENED
1	Social Isolation	8/14/2000

MANIFESTATIONS OF THE PROBLEM
What behaviors describes the problem?

Mrs. Jones locks herself inside her darkened bedroom for two days. She curls up in the corner of her room and pulls a blanket over her head.

LONG TERM GOAL
How can the patient demonstrate that they can be safely discharged?

LTG #		TARGET DATE
1	Mrs. Jones will be able to explain how feelings of depression "triggers" her social isolation and affects her relationships.	8/21/00

SHORT TERM GOAL
What intermediate step will be used to measure progress toward discharge goal?

STG #		TARGET DATE
1	Mrs. Jones will be able to verbalize the correlation between depression and social isolation.	8/17/00

#	INTERVENTIONS

List who is responsible for this intervention by name and discipline	List the modality, milieu or treatment group used to do the intervention	Describe the focus of the intervention and the expected result of participation	List the frequency of the intervention

CHAPTER 8 SELF-TEST

Answer the following questions. When you have completed the test, check your answers in Appendix B.

1. What is a long-term goal?

2. What is a short-term goal?

3. What are three reasons for having short-term goals?

4. What does the therapist/treatment team define as long-term goals?

5. What are the four possible treatment outcomes for long-term goals?

The journey of a thousand miles begins with one step . . . — **Lao-Tzu**

You have to stop to change directions. — **Erich Fromm**

Interventions

WHAT IS THE STAFF'S ROLE IN TREATMENT?

CMS requirements state, "The team must lay out all planned modalities that will be used to treat the patient while they are hospitalized." ☞ B122

"Having identified the problems requiring treatment, and defining outcome goals to be achieved, appropriate treatment approaches must be identified." ☞ B122

An intervention is the part of the treatment plan that specifies what the treatment team will do to help the patient gain insight into, and work toward, the resolution of his or her problems. Unlike goals, which outline what the patient is to accomplish, interventions clearly state what the *staff* will do to help the patient achieve his or her treatment goals.

Interventions are based on the length of stay and the level of care. Interventions for clients in outpatient, long-term therapy will have a different focus and intensity than those for patients in a hospital setting.

Think of the treatment plan as a map. The therapist/treatment team has charted all the streets and highways by doing assessments, and now they are going to help the patient choose the roads that will get them where they want to go.

In order to arrive at the destination, the team has to help patients learn to deal with the roadblocks that crop up along the journey. Once the patient knows where these pitfalls are and how to either avoid or manage them, the patient stands a better chance of arriving in one piece. Teaching patients to circumnavigate the roadblocks is what interventions are all about.

Not all patients will choose the same road to recovery. Therefore, the therapist/treatment team will have to design a set of varied treatment experiences, utilizing different treatment approaches that will help the patient learn to deal with his or her problems. The different approaches or complementary learning experiences will be discipline specific and point out several techniques and alternatives to teach the patient how to deal with a single problem.

It is not enough for the staff to delineate what therapy or modality they will use to treat the problem. It is imperative that the treatment team and the patient know the purpose or focus of that activity. In other words, does the patient understand what he or she is supposed to learn from this specific therapy?

Almost all treatment units post scheduled unit activities and therapies. Often, patients go from group to group, not for a specific therapeutic purpose but because the schedule says it is time to go to that group.

"It must be clear . . . that the treatment received by the patient is internally consistent and not simply a series of disconnected specific modalities delivered within certain scheduled intervals." ☞ B122

Patients need to know how participation in a specific therapy is supposed to help them get better. It is not enough for the team to tell a patient that he or she is going to group therapy to encourage socialization. The patient needs to understand the benefits of social activities and what part they will play in recovery.

If the patient has poor social skills, the treatment team needs to help the patient understand how that has affected his or her life. After the patient gains insight into the problem, the treatment team or therapist can help the patient develop new techniques to approach social situations. These specific activities, evidenced by some form of measurable behavioral change, make for good interventions.

Clarity is the issue. Why should a patient go to a therapy session if he or she does not know the purpose of the therapy? Interventions spell out why a patient is in a specific therapy.

Four distinct details must be included in each intervention to ensure that it is useful in treatment.

1. *Person Responsible.* Each intervention must identify, by name and discipline, the individual on the treatment team who is primarily responsible for ensuring compliance with particular aspects (i.e., interventions) of the patient's individualized treatment program. (See B123 of the CMS.)
2. *Modality.* The treatment team or therapist must identify the therapeutic modality, milieu, or treatment group where the intervention is accomplished. (See B122 of the CMS.)
3. *Focus.* The intervention must describe the focus of the intervention and what the patient is to gain from attending the therapy. (See B122 of the CMS.)
4. *Frequency.* The team or therapist must specify how often the specific treatment modality is done. (See B122 of the CMS.)

This level of specificity can make treatment professionals uncomfortable. People are often uncomfortable with accountability, but it's a crucial part of the process because the patient is at stake. Therapeutic accountability leads to treatment success and ultimately is a key factor in whether the patient will get better.

The therapist is responsible for finding a way to help the patient improve. We will discuss outcomes in Chapter 12, but for now, you should know that these requirements are not only part of the CMS conditions of participation, but also the right thing to do.

As previously discussed, the treatment team needs to rely on the assessment of the patient's strengths and abilities so that they become the basis for choosing effective interventions.

For instance, if a patient is intelligent, the use of cognitive-based therapies might be appropriate. If a patient is good at expressing his or her thoughts and feelings, emotive types of interventions might be the correct choice. Using peer pressure is a wonderful therapeutic tool for dealing with denial.

It is important to remember that a trait is not necessarily a strength. Although the term *asset* is often used interchangeably with *strength*, assets are personal strengths that can be used by the treatment team to help a patient solve his or her problems.

Build on the patient's assets to deal with his or her weaknesses. Again, a major factor in any successful treatment plan is the ability of the therapist/treatment team to assess the patient's assets and harness those assets to be used as a basis for therapeutic interventions in the treatment plan.

Remember, outside forces can be patient assets. If the therapist can engage the client's employer or family to positively affect a treatment outcome, they represent a patient asset.

Let's explore the use of interventions in our model treatment plan.

Problem Statement: Social Isolation

MANIFESTATION:

Ms. Jones locked herself inside a darkened bedroom for two days. She curls up in the corner of her room and pulls a blanket over her head.

LONG-TERM GOAL:

Ms. Jones will be able to explain how her depression triggers her social isolation and affects her relationships.

SHORT-TERM GOAL:

Ms. Jones will be able to verbalize the correlation between depression and social isolation.

INTERVENTIONS:

Staff will help Ms. Jones explore the reasons she needs to isolate from her family.

The basic premise for this intervention is good, but it does not meet the assigned CMS criteria. Let us examine different items that would clarify this intervention for the staff and patient:

1. Simply stating "staff will" does not differentiate which member of the teams has responsibility for ensuring that the patient receives this therapy.
2. It does not specify what therapeutic modality is used to address this task.
3. It does not specify why Ms. Jones needs to "explore the reasons" she feels the need to isolate from her family.
4. It does not specify how often Ms. Jones will go to this therapy.

All of these things must be stated to ensure clarity in the plan.

Here is an example of this same intervention when it has been "fleshed out" and correctly written. Notice how the specificity of the intervention helps clearly delineate *what* is going to happen and *who* is responsible.

INTERVENTIONS:

Stephanie Johnson, RN, will help Ms. Jones explore and come to terms with the reasons she needs social isolation. This is accomplished by attending group therapy three times per week.

Some treatment professionals are uncomfortable with this level of specificity. The truth is, specificity makes certain individuals accountable for outcomes. Treatment professionals must recognize that they are dealing with real people and that they must take responsibility for providing the patient with therapeutic activities that give him or her the best chance at recovery. Writing with this level of specificity is not only required by the CMS guidelines, but also represents good treatment!

It has been argued that some staff will feel more comfortable with a plan that specifies their therapeutic tasks. Earlier, we discussed the fact that people sometimes fail when they do not know what is expected from them. A specific plan can be of great value to the patient and the therapist.

Interventions should use discipline-specific approaches to help a patient gain the skills to deal with his or her problems. Let us examine another intervention that would help our fictitious patient resolve her social isolation.

We used the first intervention to help her gain insight; now let us help her to test that insight in the treatment milieu.

INTERVENTIONS:

Larry Walker, OTR, will help Ms. Jones develop a list of likes and dislikes, to create a specific program to engage her in unit activities with other patients. This is to be done in an individual session by 3/8/04.

In this intervention, the occupational therapist is simply getting Ms. Jones to delineate the activities she feels she could tolerate. Verbal praise or other forms of positive reinforcement are used as tools to help Ms. Jones accomplish her goals.

Let us examine a different kind of intervention, one that requires a team effort to accomplish. Here is an example of an intervention that cannot be completed by a single member of the treatment team.

INTERVENTIONS:

Staff will place patient on suicidal precautions.

Here is an area of great concern. Treatment facilities often use this intervention to ensure that the patient is watched and that his or her safety is maintained. Often, mental health workers and aides know that suicidal precautions mean that they should observe the patient on a regular basis. What they do not know is what specific types of behaviors they should be monitoring. Further, if they should happen to see these behaviors, what should they do about it?

Additionally, it is impossible for one person to do an intervention 24 hours a day, 7 days a week. So how can the treatment team overcome these obstacles? Writing an appropriate intervention is a good start. Compare the following intervention to the previous example.

INTERVENTIONS:

Stephanie Johnson, RN, will instruct the treatment team that Ms. Jones has been placed on Q15 checks for suicidal precautions. Charge nurses will instruct staff to ensure a safe environment free of dangerous implements and to observe Ms. Jones for signs of agitation, irritability, sadness, or other indications of suicidal thought, reassuring her that she is safe and redirecting her attention away from detrimental behavior or thought. Staff will report any untoward behaviors to the charge nurse. This is to be done PRN [pro re nata, Latin for *as the need arises*] in daily unit activity.

Stephanie Johnson, RN, is still responsible for ensuring that the patient receives this intervention, but she has appropriately delegated the function to other levels of staff. The trick is to delegate with enough information to ensure success. Tell the staff what they are to look for and help them understand what they should do if the patient needs staff intervention. It is important to remember that even though the RN has entrusted patient observation to other staff, it is still being carried out under the auspices of the RN's license and authority. If something goes wrong, the person holding the license and authority (the RN) is responsible.

As you can see, interventions run the gambit of patient possibilities. Good therapists identify the proper therapeutic focus of their patient's planned interventions so that the intervention will produce a specific desired treatment outcome.

Beyond any doubt, good intervention is a basic element for successful outcomes.

Figure 9.1 is an example of a completed problem resolution plan.

Figure 9.1 | Problem Resolution Plan

	Problem Resolution Plan	Jones, Mrs. Ida Lee DOB 11/07/1918 Religious Preference: Catholic Marital Status: Married Admit Date: 8/7/2000 Attending Physician: Dr. Landman
		Addressograph Imprint

PROBLEM #	PROBLEM STATEMENT	DATE OPENED
1	Social Isolation	8/14/2000

MANIFESTATIONS OF THE PROBLEM
What behaviors describes the problem?

Mrs. Jones locks herself inside her darkened bedroom for two days. She curls up in the corner of her room and pulls a blanket over her head.

LONG TERM GOAL
How can the patient demonstrate that they can be safely discharged?

LTG #		TARGET DATE
1	Mrs. Jones will be able to explain how feelings of depression "triggers" her social isolation and effects her relationships.	8/21/00

SHORT TERM GOAL
What intermediate step will be used to measure progress toward discharge goal?

STG #		TARGET DATE
1	Mrs. Jones will be able to verbalize the correlation between depression and social isolation.	8/17/00

#	INTERVENTIONS
	Stephanie Johnson, RN, will instruct the treatment team that Mrs. Jones has been placed on Q15 checks for suicidal precautions. Charge nurses will instruct staff to observe Mrs. Jones for signs of agitation, irritability, sadness, or other indications of suicidal thought and redirect her toward positive thought as necessary. This is to be done PRN (as needed) in daily unit activity.

List who is responsible for this intervention by name and discipline	List the modality, milieu or treatment group used to do the intervention	Describe the focus of the intervention and the expected result of participation	List the frequency of the intervention

CHAPTER 9 SELF-TEST

Answer the following questions. When you have completed the test, check your answers in Appendix B.

1. Why delineate interventions?

2. What are the four areas of specificity in a good intervention?

3. Who benefits from good interventions?

4. Why is it important to name the person responsible for ensuring that the intervention is completed?

5. Why should a licensed person be careful when delegating the day-to-day function of an intervention?

*Action and reaction, ebb and flow, trial and error,
change . . . this is the rhythm of our living.*
— **Bruce Barton**

Nothing in progression can rest on its original plan.
— **Edmund Burke**

Documentation and Updates | 10

HOW DO WE MEASURE PATIENT PROGRESS?

No battle plan survives the first shot! Plans grow and change according to patient progress—or lack of progress. How do we measure the success of our treatment plan? By constantly monitoring and documenting the patient's progress and changing the plan when the patient completes goals, or fails to make progress toward recovery. This process keeps the plan alive and that is the essence of a good treatment plan. To have successful treatment outcomes, we must create a living, breathing document that changes as necessary to maintain active treatment of the patient.

Measuring Progress

An interdisciplinary treatment team addresses the patient's problems using many perspectives. The treatment plan delineates the responsibilities of each member of the treatment team. Each intervention is then individualized to tell us who is going to oversee the process, how often it is going to be done, and what treatment modality is going to be used to address the problem.

CMS requires that each discipline must report on the success of its plan of interventions and the progress the patient has made toward alleviating any problems and meeting goals. We track this progress using daily progress notes.

We specifically document the progress made in everyday treatment and unit activities by "charting to problems." CMS demands that treatment notes relate to the treatment plan, and spell out what "the hospital staff is doing to carry out the treatment plan and the patient's response to the interventions." ☞ B124 The goal is to ensure that there is "adequate documentation to justify the diagnosis and the treatment and the rehabilitation activities carried out." ☞ B124

CMS says that "the treatment received by the patient must be documented in such a way to assure that all active therapeutic efforts are included." ☞ B125

Surveyors will measure the presence of active treatment by asking a series of questions called *probes*. Probes are specific questions created to discern what the staff and patient understand about the treatment plan; they determine if clients and therapists agree about the choice of problems and therapies. Here are some CMS probes related to documentation:

- Are the treatment notes relative to the identified problems?
- Are the treatment notes indicative of the patient's response to treatment?
- Do the progress notes relate to specific patient problems or progress?

These standards lead up to CMS's defining treatment statement:

Active treatment is an essential requirement for inpatient psychiatric care. Active treatment is a clinical process involving the ongoing assessment, diagnosis, intervention, evaluation of care, and treatment and planning under the direction of a psychiatrist.

Realistically, what CMS (and good common sense) demands is that we actively monitor our patient's progress and response to our treatment. We also want to be sure that our patients understand (to the fullest extent possible) their therapies and the need for treatment.

Our goal is to see that patients receive as much meaningful therapy as possible to do the greatest good. When it comes down to a survey, the documentation in the patient's chart is the *only means* to provide evidence that the staff is actively carrying out the patient's plan of care.

Charting Progress Notes

The first step in documenting effective treatment is called charting. A progress note is used to documents the patient's response to the care he or she is provided and is used to document how the patient reacted to specific therapies. Because a patient's record is called a chart, the act of writing in the chart is called *charting* or *clinical charting*.

When staff charts a progress note, they begin by listing the problem number from the problem list. This system indicates the progress of staff interventions related to specific problems. If the first problem the treatment team identified for treatment was social isolation it would be labeled number one (1) and all notes related to this specific problem would be labeled with the number one (1) as well. Notes related to the second problem on the list would be annotated with the number two (2) and so forth. If you learn nothing else from this chapter, remember this:

SURVEYOR'S RULE NUMBER ONE

If it hasn't been documented, it hasn't been done.

Proper documentation is essential. The therapist's intent or actual deeds do not count legally during the survey process unless they have been documented. You must properly document your actions for them to become legal and valid. Beyond this rule, documentation is extremely important for several reasons:

- Documentation proves the involvement of each discipline in the care of the patient.
- Documentation provides a clear picture of patient progress, or lack of progress, for all staff to read and monitor.
- In an increasingly litigious environment, good documentation is the best safeguard against lawsuits.
- Documentation will also help assure compliance with accreditation and licensing requirements.
- Documentation will justify and verify the bill for treatment.
- Accountability reviews of charting are increasing. Insurance companies will and do deny claims based on improper documentation.

However, the most important reason is monitoring quality patient care. Good charting will help the therapist monitor these issues:

1. Did the treatment team document that the patient received the care that the plan says he or she was supposed to get?
2. Was the plan updated as necessary to ensure patient progress?

Having said all of this, the reverse is also true: *documentation is not the same thing as treatment*. The rule applies to documenting an event rather than whether treatment took place. Most clients never see their records and never really think about seeing them. The therapist should strive to provide documentation in a concise fashion and to write notes that record enough information to both properly manage the patient and meet regulatory agency requirements.

There are many styles and formats for clinical charting. Charting styles and requirements will vary from hospital to hospital and setting to setting. This workbook will not suggest a specific format (e.g., SOAP, Narrative, Omaha, Charting by Exception) for clinical charting, nor debate the relative merits of these different charting styles. There are however, some basic rules that all charting must follow.

In order to assign proper credit to the different disciplines, each patient progress note should begin with the following information.

1. Date
2. Time
3. Problem number

It is also essential that each note is signed and lists the discipline of the individual who wrote the note.

It is also very important in the current fiscal environment to ensure charting substance. The chart should provide a chronological record of the patient's progress. Specifically, progress notes should relate to the identified patient problems and the patient's progress toward the treatment plan's goals.

Clinical charting or treatment notes "that state, 'Patient slept well,' or 'no complaints' constitute observations and do not indicate how the patient is responding to treatment and progressing toward set goals." ☞ B126

Team members must record their interpretation of specific behavior manifestations related to progress and goals. After all, if the patient "slept well" and had "no complaints," why does he or she need to be in treatment?

In addition, although it is accepted practice to increase the frequency of charting during patient crisis, it is equally important to note:

The frequency of the note is not the primary indicator of good care.

"The frequency of the progress notes is determined by the condition of the patient but must be recorded at least weekly for the first 2 months and at least once a month thereafter". ☞ B130

In reality, the facility's policies, bylaws or rules and regulations will dictate how often a staff member will be required to make a progress note. However, during an inpatient hospitalization, most surveyors will not accept anything less than charting three times per week by primary team members. Specifically, the staff should chart after each specific therapy session.

Treatment Plan Updates

Treatment teams must set aside time for all disciplines, under the direction of a psychiatrist, to gather, evaluate and report on their view of patient needs and progress. Progress or lack of progress toward treatment goals are reviewed and *updated* as necessary at this meeting.

Each discipline must monitor its portion of the patient's treatment, as well as the success of its particular interventions in the patient's recovery. Progress toward treatment goals and patient problem resolution is the focus of this meeting.

Whenever possible, patients or family members and caregivers must be included in treatment team meetings. The long-term success of treatment depends on their participation.

There seems to be a great deal of confusion about when a team has to have treatment plan update meetings. Actually, CMS has no set timeframe for treatment team updates. Rather, they provide points in treatment that would necessitate these meetings. Treatment teams must meet and discuss revisions to a patient's plan when:

- The patient achieves a goal.
- The patient fails to make progress toward a goal.
- A new problem is identified.
- A problem is dropped from the treatment plan.

Patients must be aware of their plan for treatment and their role and responsibilities in getting better. During a treatment plan update meeting, the team considers and documents any changes to the plan on the treatment team update sheet, including information regarding:

- The status of each problem.
- Whether there are any new problems.
- The appropriateness of the long-term and short-term goals.
- Whether the interventions are working or whether new interventions should be included in the plan.
- The viability of the target dates for achieving the various components of the plan.

The team documents this update session on both the treatment team update sheet (the problem resolution plan update) and the treatment team signature sheet. See Figures 10.1 and 10.2 for copies of an example form for each of these tasks.

Treatment Team Signature Sheet

A treatment team signature sheet is required to document the treatment team and update meetings. Basic information should include:

- The signature of the physician who approved and ordered the new plan of care.
- The date and time of the meeting.
- An indication (signature or initial and discipline) of all the treatment team members attending the meeting.
- The patient's, family members, or caregiver's level of participation in the planning process.
- The patient's, family members, or caregiver's signature documenting his or her participation.

Without this paper trail, no one can prove the participation and involvement of the team members, patient, or family and caregivers in the treatment process. The treatment team/therapist should complete and sign signature sheets for each update meeting.

Figure 10.1 | Problem Resolution Plan Update

Problem Resolution Plan Update

Addressograph Imprint

PROBLEM NUMBER	PROBLEM STATUS	☐ CONTINUED	☐ DEFERRED	☐ REVISED	☐ CLOSED
	LTG # _____	☐ CONTINUED	☐ DEFERRED	☐ REVISED	☐ CLOSED
	STG # _____	☐ CONTINUED	☐ DEFERRED	☐ REVISED	☐ CLOSED

PROBLEM NAME _____ DATE _____/_____/_____

_____
_____
_____
_____
_____
_____

PROBLEM NUMBER	PROBLEM STATUS	☐ CONTINUED	☐ DEFERRED	☐ REVISED	☐ CLOSED
	LTG # _____	☐ CONTINUED	☐ DEFERRED	☐ REVISED	☐ CLOSED
	STG # _____	☐ CONTINUED	☐ DEFERRED	☐ REVISED	☐ CLOSED

PROBLEM NAME _____ DATE _____/_____/_____

_____
_____
_____
_____
_____

PROBLEM NUMBER	PROBLEM STATUS	☐ CONTINUED	☐ DEFERRED	☐ REVISED	☐ CLOSED
	LTG # _____	☐ CONTINUED	☐ DEFERRED	☐ REVISED	☐ CLOSED
	STG # _____	☐ CONTINUED	☐ DEFERRED	☐ REVISED	☐ CLOSED

PROBLEM NAME _____ DATE _____/_____/_____

_____
_____
_____
_____
_____
_____

Figure 10.2 | Treatment Team/Patient Signature Sheet

Addressograph Imprint	**Treatment Team / Patient Signature Sheet**

☐ Initial Planning Session   ☐ Initial Treatment Team   ☐ Planning Update   ☐ Administrative

The Following Team Members Participated in the Interdisciplinary Treatment Plans, Reviews or Updates

Attending Physician: _____

Case Manager: _____

Social Worker: _____

Psychologist: _____

Activity Therapy: _____

Nursing: _____

_____

Other Allied Professional: _____

_____

_____

ATTENTION

PATIENT / FAMILY INVOLVEMENT

This plan has been explained to the patient or appropriate other person.
The patient or other appropriate person has been give the opportunity to ask questions and participate in the plan for their care as documented below.

My signature attests to my participation in treatment planning and correctly documents my level of participation

☐ Contributed to Goals and Plan   ☑ Present at Team Meeting   ☐ Unable to Participate

☐ Aware of Plan and Contract   ☐ Refused to Participate   ☐ Refused to Sign Plan

Patient Signature _Mrs. Ida Lee Jones_____   Date _8_ | _24_ | _00_

Family Member's Signature _Daniel W. Jones_____   Date _8_ | _24_ | _00_

CHAPTER 10 SELF-TEST

Answer the following questions. When you have completed the test, check your answers in Appendix B.

1. How do we measure a patient's progress toward treatment goals?

2. How often are you required to have a treatment team update meeting?

3. What are the required parts of a progress note?

4. What is the purpose of a treatment team signature sheet?

5. What old treatment axiom is Surveyor's Rule Number One?

6. How would you define *active treatment*?

7. What patient situations would necessitate a treatment team update meeting?

Learning is either a continuing thing or it is nothing.
— **Frank Tyger**

You're not here to get well . . . just better.
— **Daniel W. Johnson**

Discharge Planning

THE ABCs OF TREATMENT

As we have discussed in previous chapters, the treatment process has undergone a tremendous change. The greatest change is the amount of time a therapist has to care for his or her patient in a treatment setting.

For the most part, patients do not participate in treatment to get well; they go to get better. The trick is to improve the patient's well being so that he or she can move to a lower level of care. The days of 28-day alcoholism programs and 1-year community psychiatric programs are over.

Criteria for admission and managed care have severely limited access and shortened treatment time for all patients. Therapists no longer have the luxury of doing long-term therapy in any treatment settings.

For most providers, therapy has become a crisis intervention, or ABC model of treatment:

- A—Assess the patient
- B—Band-Aid the blockages
- C—Continue the care in a less restrictive environment

When the patient and mental health professions understand these changes, the expectations for treatment are dramatically altered. Treatment changes from an inpatient therapy model to a crisis management and referral system model. Planning the patient's continued care in an outpatient setting becomes critical to his or her recovery.

The primary reason for patient relapse is noncompliance. Whether that means the patient is not following an identified aftercare program or not taking his or her medications is irrelevant. What is relevant is that this age-old problem is a major portion of what is visibly wrong with mental health treatment today.

The majority of mental health patients in America today suffer from chronic mental illness. When they are unable to cope with the outside pressures, they retreat to a protected environment for help.

In most cases, patients dramatically improve in this treatment environment, because they are protected by a cocoon of physicians, nurses, or therapists who tend to their needs and safety. The old saying, "Three hots and a cot" goes a long way. In other words, putting the patient in a protected

Figure 11.1 | Psychiatric Circle of Life

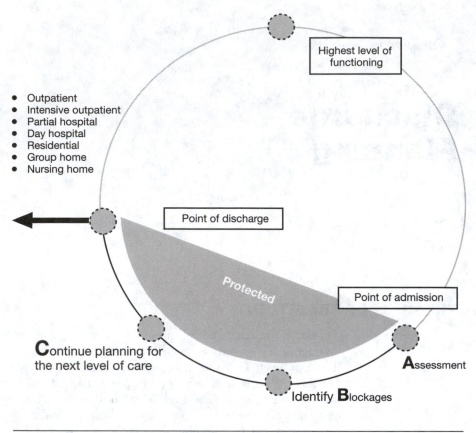

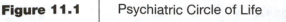

environment where his or her needs are being met 24 hours a day would make almost anyone feel and function better.

In this less-than-ideal treatment environment, patients nevertheless improve because they are in a protected environment. The only real chance they have to successfully function out side of a particular level of care is good discharge planning.

In 1995, discharge planning became the third special condition of participation in the Medicare and Medicaid programs.

Essentially, CMS recognized that short lengths of stay necessitated more aggressive planning for movement to the next level of care. There is also another advantage to this arrangement: it is less costly. The use of any therapeutic environment on the continuum, other than inpatient treatment, almost always reduces the cost of treatment. Partial hospitals cost less than hospitals, outpatient care cost less than residential care, and so forth. Therefore, moving patients to a less restrictive environment became another cost-control measure.

Shorter inpatient lengths of stay necessitated earlier discharge planning. Discharge planning has essentially become a parallel component to any treatment environment. Specifically, the goal for each level of care in the continuum is to prepare the patient to move on to a lower (less restrictive) level of service.

CMS guidelines for the survey process state, "the record of each patient who has been discharged must have a discharge summary that includes a recapitulation of the patient's hospitalization." ☞ B133

The discharge summary should contain several specific pieces of information:

1. "The record of each patient who has been discharged should indicate the extent to which goals established in the patient's treatment plan have been met." ⌒ B133
2. "A recapitulation of the patient's hospitalization" ⌒ B133
3. "A summary of the circumstances and rationale for admission" ⌒ B133
4. "A baseline of the psychiatric, physical and social functioning of the patient at the time of discharge" ⌒ B133
5. "Evidence of the patient/family response to the treatment interventions" ⌒ B133

The purpose for this summary of care is to help the therapist who will do follow-up or aftercare gain insight into the recently completed treatment process. Why should each level of care have to start over with the patient's treatment? As you move a patient through the continuum of care, pass on what you have learned. Document what therapeutically worked in the current level of care so that the therapists can use knowledge and insight from previous treatment and not waste time learning how to solve the same problems in the current level of care. Remember:

In a continuum of care, the current treatment of specific problems is continued in a new level of care, with a different focus and intensity of service.

Standard B134 is the planning component of the Discharge Planning Standard. This standard asks that the discharge planner provide "recommendations from appropriate services concerning follow-up or aftercare." ⌒ B134

As we discussed earlier in this chapter, the two purposes of discharge planning are to:

1. Provide information to the treatment professionals who will be continuing the patient's treatment in the next level of the continuum of care.
2. Devise a plan of follow-up care that gives the patient the best chance for treatment success.

THE KEY TO SUCCESSFUL DISCHARGE PLANNING

The bottom line of successful discharge planning is to share information and devise ways to continue the protective treatment environment.

Where no plan has been laid, treatment is soon surrendered to chaos.

As we have discussed, most patients get better when they are actively being treated in a protected environment. Treatment professionals cannot cure a majority of the patients they treat, but most of the time, they can help them successfully function in a less restrictive environment.

"The patient's discharge summary should describe the services and supports that are appropriate to the patient's needs and that will be effective on the day of discharge." ⌒ B134 If patients are to have long-term success in recovery, the discharge plan must include:

*   "A complete description of arrangements with treatment and other community resources for the provision of follow-up services. Reference should be made to prior verbal and written communication and exchange of information;
*   A plan outlining psychiatric, medical/physical treatment, and the medications regimen as applicable;
*   Specific appointment date(s) and names and addresses of the service provider(s);
*   Description of community housing/living arrangement;
*   Economic/financial status or plan, i.e., supplemental security income benefits;

- Recreational and leisure resources; and
- A complete description of the involvement of family and significant others with the patient after discharge." ✎ B134

In order for a patient to have a chance to avoid recidivism there must be a plan. For success, that plan must detail what is going to be done to ensure that the patient can function in a progressively less restrictive therapeutic environment.

Finally, CMS requires "a brief summary of the patient's condition on discharge.

- The patient's discharge planning process should address anticipated problems after discharge and suggested means for intervention . . . .
- The discharge summary and/or plan should contain information about the status of the patient on the day of discharge, including the psychiatric, physical, and functional condition." ✎ B135

CHAPTER 11 SELF-TEST

Answer the following questions. When you have completed the test, check your answers in Appendix B.

1. What do the letters *A*, *B*, and *C* stand for in the ABC model of treatment?

2. What is the number one reason for readmission to psychiatric treatment?

3. Name two advantages to moving a patient into a lower level of care.

4. What is the purpose of a continuum of care?

5. What is the only real chance a patient has to succeed when he or she moves to a less restrictive environment?

6. What is the primary purpose of the summary in the discharge plan?

A place for everything and everything in its place.
— **Isabella Mary Beaton**

Confusion is a word we invented for an order that is not yet understood. — **Henry Miller**

Acuity and Patient Severity Scales

12

WHAT IS A PATIENT ACUITY SCALE?

Treatment teams must be able to use measurable and objective criteria to define patient progress in treatment. To accomplish this task, the treatment team must have some means of consistently measuring the patient's condition in a universal language. The measure of the severity of the patient's illness and symptoms is an acuity scale.

Acuity scales have many purposes in therapeutic settings. The primary purpose of an acuity scale is outcomes measurement. This function is closely followed by making sure that the clinical staffing is appropriate and safe. Treatment facilities need to make sure the correct number of staff and the right disciplines are present to manage the patient milieu.

The difficulty with most patient severity scales is that nurses, physicians, and therapists use subjective observation to decide where a patient "fits" on the acuity scale. The secret to success of any measurement tool is universality and continuity. Here are two examples of acuity scales currently in use and the limitations of each.

The Use of Rating Scales

Subjective ordinal scales are used to rate patient behaviors and progress based on the judgment of the therapist. This means the factors that are used to move the patient from point A to point B on the scale are entirely dependent on the therapist and the assessment of the patient's relative progress as defined by the therapist's subjective interpretation of the patient's behavior. Using this type of rating scale only correlates the patient's improvement to his or her own progress. That is, it has meaning only in the context of that individual patient.

Each patient is rated according to his or her individual circumstances and there is no connectivity between patients. Using subjective ordinal scales limits the possibility for universal interpretation of the treatment data or progress.

Simply put, the data on a subjective, ordinal scale is only meaningful to the therapist and patient for whom the scale was designed. It cannot be used as a basis to rate multiple patients with varied symptomology.

Positive and Negative Ordinal Scales

Another method would be entail using a behavioral approach to documenting patient progress. After the patient is admitted to treatment, the therapist or team takes a baseline of the target behaviors that are being treated. The treatment team documents the initial frequency count and then plots the variances in the frequency of these behaviors using a positive (for increase) or negative (for decrease) position on an ordinal scale.

To illustrate the limitations of this scale, let us assume that there are three patients undergoing concurrent treatment. One patient has a problem with lying, another with stealing, and the third with violent outbursts. For each target behavior, the treatment team will derive a baseline of occurrence.

Suppose patient #1 lied ten times per day, patient #2 stole three times per day and patient #3 had two violent outbursts per day. Because each patient has different target behaviors, in varying amounts, how will the therapist determine the correct plot point? Do one-and-a-half stealing episodes equal one lying event?

If the rating of progress is related only to the behaviors of one particular patient, universality is not possible.

The only treatment scenario that could make this scale universally effective is if all of the patients were working on the same target behavior with the same occurrence of frequency.

Here are three additional patient scenarios. Although each situation is different, there is a common thread that runs through each case. Using this common thread, the question becomes would it be possible to develop a rating system based on the intensity of the staff interventions and not on the particular patient's behaviors? If so, could the staff universally apply this scale to other patients?

PATIENT #1

The hospital admitted patient A when he came into the ER after an overdose (OD). He was extremely distraught because his wife was having an affair and told him she wanted a divorce. The patient repeatedly stated, "I have nothing to live for and I want to die."

PATIENT #2

The police brought patient B to the Emergency Room (ER) after he threatened to jump off a building. He states, "I hear voices telling me to jump of a building and kill myself. They just don't stop." The staff admits the patient to the hospital.

PATIENT #3

Patient C is an alcoholic. He is admitted with an extremely high blood alcohol level and needs medical detoxification. His vital signs are very unstable and his medical condition is critical.

What is the common thread that runs through all three cases? Although all three patients are severely ill, none of them exhibits the same behaviors or has the same symptomology. Yet, they all are in need of inpatient care because they are in imminent danger of harm or loss of life.

The common thread in each of these patients is their need for constant interventions to protect their lives. The events that precipitated their need for protection are varied, but their need for protection is universal.

Defining Severity Using the Intensity and Focus of Staff Interventions

By definition, the hospital is a treatment environment that provides active nursing, medical and therapeutic interventions 24 hours a day, 7 days a week. It is the most intense treatment environment possible.

In order to be admitted to a hospital, the patient must need the highest level of medical or psychiatric intervention. Although all three of the patients in this illustration have different problem manifestations, all three need protection! In this case, we can measure patient severity by the intensity of the staff intervention. Each patient needs the protection of a hospital environment to manage a life-threatening situation. The severity of the problem is at its apex.

Once we define severity using the intensity and focus of the staff interventions, universality is possible.

Patient severity is based on the intensity of the staff's interventions and not on patient behaviors.

Hence, protecting a patient who is a danger to himself or herself or others is the first and most intense universally defined point on the severity/acuity scale. Protecting the patient is the major focus of staff interventions.

Now that we have a starting point on our severity scale, the key will be to break down treatment into defined tasks that move the patient toward a less intense, lower level of care.

STAGES OF RECOVERY

All patients go through *stages of recovery*. Inpatient treatment interventions begin with protecting the patient and moves toward discharge. As patients move toward discharge, the intensity of staff interventions changes and decreases. These changes are predictable and based on the current level of the severity and intensity of patient management. As treatment progresses, the staff can choose to move the patient to a lower level of care. (See Figure 12.1)

How do we know when to change the level of care? *The intensity of care, combined with the treatment focus* determines the benchmark of patient progress toward discharge. At some point, a less intense setting will be adequate to continue the therapeutic interventions. The job of the therapist is to determine where this point is for the patient.

Although there are a multitude of diagnoses, and even more problem statements, all patients go through similar stages of recovery and in the same order. Chapter 1 stated that:

People seek treatment when they become overwhelmed and lack the capacity to deal with their problems.

The patient's inability to manage life's pressures in his or her current environment constitutes the need for a protected environment.

Stage One: Protect

During stage one of recovery, the patient admits that his or her life is out of control and abdicates some of his or her freedom, in return for the safety of a protected environment (asylum). Therefore, the first treatment task is to protect the patient.

Figure 12.1 | Hierarchy of treatment intensity

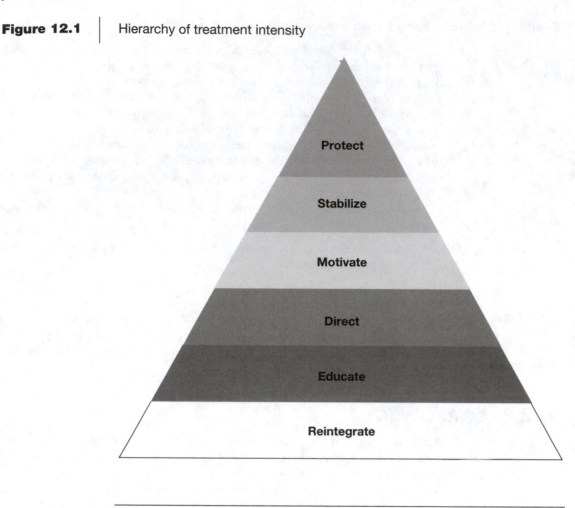

Stage Two: Stabilize

If the team does a good job of initial crisis management, the patient will stabilize. This in no way means that the patient is ready for discharge; rather it means the patient is no longer in imminent danger. When the patient becomes stable, he or she crosses the threshold into the second stage of recovery, which is stabilization.

Stage Three: Motivate

The next stage of recovery is to motivate the patient to deal with his or her problems. Most patients recognize the need to get better, but in order to begin recovery they have to want to get well. The purpose of motivating a patient is to give him or her insight into his or her problems and to make him or her *want* to get better. The third therapeutic intervention we do for a patient in treatment is to motivate him or her to want to get better.

Stage Four: Direct

Once a patient has the desire to get better, he or she will begin to ask, "OK, what do I do now?" Because managed care has severely limited the time the treatment team has to treat a patient, therapy has become increasingly more directive oriented. The therapist tells the patient what to do to begin recovery and then helps him or her move on! This process of directing the patient toward recuperation is the next stage of recovery.

Our fourth task, then, is to start the patient on the path to recovery by giving him or her direction. At this point in treatment the patient:

- Is out of danger,
- Feels better,
- Wants to recover, and
- Knows what he or she must do to begin recovery.

The next question is, "How do I do that?"

Stage Five: Educate

The next segment on the road to recovery is to teach the patient what he or she has to know to deal with issues in a home or less restrictive environment.

The therapist cannot expect a patient to deal with an incomprehensible problem or disease. The treatment team cannot just tell the patient how to recover, he or she must be taught new coping skills and techniques to use in the real world.

Helping patients understand different therapeutic techniques or finding new coping skills is what stage five of recovery is all about. Patient education is a powerful tool in therapeutic recovery.

Stage Six: Reintegrate

Educating the patient is not enough. Patients say, "I understand what I need to do, but you don't live in my neighborhood," or "Try that at my house."

After the patient is taught to use the proper therapeutic tools and the new coping skills needed to begin recovery, the therapist must teach the patient to apply these skills in his or her home community. This discharge process is reintegration.

The intensity of staff intervention decreases as the patient travels through the stages of recovery. In all cases, the staff moves the client through the same therapeutic levels of care regardless of the individual patient symptomology. We can gauge a patient's progress toward recovery based on the intensity of the level of staff interventions. *How long* a patient remains in each stage of recovery will vary in relation to his or her problems and needs.

Now that we have defined the stages of recovery, we can use these points to create a universal acuity scale. A "10" on the universal acuity scale represents the most intense focus of treatment. Each succeeding stage of recovery is represented by a decreasing value until all of the acuity scale is defined.

Since each stage of treatment is less intense and moving toward recovery, we can plot patient progress using these universal definitions.

10–9 Point One—Protect

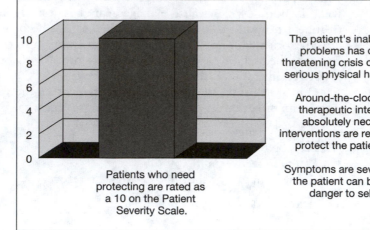

The patient's inability to manage problems has created a life-threatening crisis or situation where serious physical harm is imminent.

Around-the-clock nursing and therapeutic interventions are absolutely necessary. Staff interventions are regularly needed to protect the patient from harm.

Symptoms are severe enough that the patient can be defined as a danger to self or others.

Patients who need protecting are rated as a 10 on the Patient Severity Scale.

EXAMPLES OF POSSIBLE BEHAVIORS AND PROBLEMS

- Aggressive behavior
- Anorexia
- Compulsive ritualistic behavior
- Confusion
- Paranoid delusions
- Drug/food interaction
- Disorientation
- Erratic emotional displays
- Setting fires
- Flight of Ideas
- Hallucinations (auditory, tactile, visual)
- High risk for trauma
- Inability to communicate
- Serious medical problems
- Obsessive thoughts
- Panic attacks
- Potential for falling
- Suicide attempt
- Self-mutilating behavior
- Psychomotor agitation
- Recurrent thoughts of death
- Self-care deficit
- Self-destructive behavior
- Seizures
- Sexual abuse (active)
- Persistent suicidal ideation

As you can see, each of these problems requires immediate intervention to remove the patient from harm. Protecting a patient is the highest intensity of staff intervention, therefore the universal acuity scale starts its high point here where the intensity of staff intervention is at its greatest.

Let us now examine the types of therapeutic interventions a treatment team might employ to deal with these therapeutic issues.

EXAMPLES OF STAFF INTERVENTIONS

- Assessments (medical, psycho-social, dietary, OTR)
- Medication therapy
- Close observations
- Orienting patient
- Seclusion and restraint
- 1:1 medical or nursing therapy
- Suicide contracts
- Education about specific treatments
- Careful verbal exchanges between staff and patients— concrete, simple explanations; quiet, unhurried presentation, etc.
- Verbal assurances
- Expressive therapies
- Deescalation techniques
- Refocusing techniques
- Relaxation techniques

8–7 Point Two—Stabilize

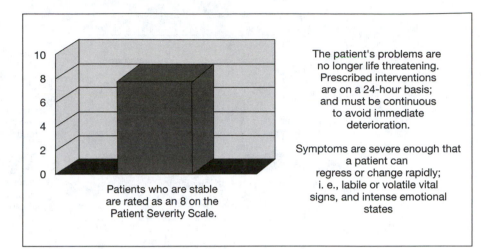

The patient's problems are no longer life threatening. Prescribed interventions are on a 24-hour basis; and must be continuous to avoid immediate deterioration.

Symptoms are severe enough that a patient can regress or change rapidly; i. e., labile or volatile vital signs, and intense emotional states

Patients who are stable are rated as an 8 on the Patient Severity Scale.

EXAMPLES OF POSSIBLE BEHAVIORS AND PROBLEMS

- Anhedonia
- Anxiety
- Anger
- Apathy
- Blunted flat affect
- Dangerous behavior
- Distorted perception of self
- Diabetes
- Fears
- Functional decline
- Hopelessness
- Helplessness
- Impulsive family/ relationship issues
- Mood swings
- Pessimism

- Poverty of speech
- Rationalization
- Self-pity
- Social withdrawal/isolation
- Seizures
- Self-consciousness
- Intense situational stress
- Unresolved grief
- Persistent unrealistic worry
- Feelings of worthlessness
- Sexual abuse (active)
- Delusions
- Paranoia
- Suicidal thoughts
- Recurrent thoughts of death

At this level, the problems continue to be critical issues, but the intensity of the problem and the staff intervention has decreased. As an example, the problem statement "suicidal thought" listed under "Stable" is less severe than "suicidal attempt" listed under "Protect." Both problems require treatment in an inpatient environment. However, the methods and intensity of dealing with protecting a patient who is actively suicidal is significantly more intense than treating a patient who is just thinking about suicide.

EXAMPLES OF STAFF INTERVENTIONS

- Medication therapy
- Desensitization
- Close observations
- Unit structure
- 1:1 therapies
- Behavioral contracts

- Education about treatment
- Group, psychotherapy, and other talk therapies
- Leisure skills groups
- Relaxation techniques/therapy
- Cognitive retraining exercises

6–5 Point Three—Motivate

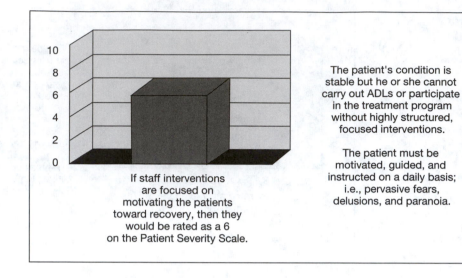

If staff interventions are focused on motivating the patients toward recovery, then they would be rated as a 6 on the Patient Severity Scale.

The patient's condition is stable but he or she cannot carry out ADLs or participate in the treatment program without highly structured, focused interventions.

The patient must be motivated, guided, and instructed on a daily basis; i.e., pervasive fears, delusions, and paranoia.

EXAMPLES OF POSSIBLE BEHAVIORS AND PROBLEMS

- Anhedonia
- Anxiety
- Anger
- Blunted flat affect
- Distorted perception of self
- Fears
- Hopelessness
- Helplessness
- Family/relationship issues
- Mood swings
- Pessimism
- Poverty of speech
- Rationalization
- Self-pity
- Social withdrawal/isolation
- Intense situational stress
- Unresolved grief
- Persistent unrealistic worry
- Feelings of worthlessness
- Intense unexpressed feelings
- Chronic feelings of emptiness or boredom

As you can see, the problems have become even less critical. The intensity of the problem and subsequent focus of staff interventions has lessened. The probability that this problem continues to be a blockage (a reason that the patient cannot be discharged) to discharge is greatly diminished.

As treatment progresses, the intensity of service may no longer justify the need for inpatient hospitalization. At this stage of treatment, the staff should think about moving the patient into the next level in the continuum of care. If the remaining therapeutic work on this problem can be treated effectively in a lower intensity setting, the "blockage to discharge" is gone. This problem, on its own, is no longer a barrier to discharge.

EXAMPLES OF STAFF INTERVENTIONS

- Medication therapy
- 1:1 therapies
- Behavioral contracts
- Education about treatment
- Group, psychotherapy, and other talk therapies
- Leisure skills groups
- Milieu management/ structured unit activity
- Peer pressure/support
- Family therapy

4–3 Point Four—Direct

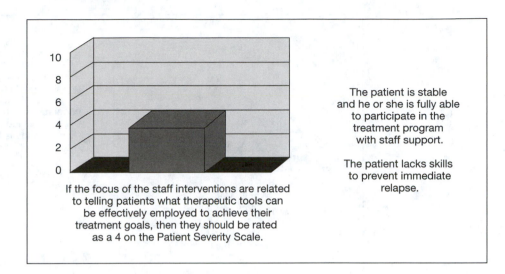

If the focus of the staff interventions are related to telling patients what therapeutic tools can be effectively employed to achieve their treatment goals, then they should be rated as a 4 on the Patient Severity Scale.

The patient is stable and he or she is fully able to participate in the treatment program with staff support.

The patient lacks skills to prevent immediate relapse.

EXAMPLES OF POSSIBLE BEHAVIORS AND PROBLEMS

- Academic deficit
- Apathy
- Chronic feeling of emptiness
- Boredom
- Disorganization
- Daytime sleepiness
- Fatigue
- Family/relationship issues
- Mood swings
- Pessimism
- Poor judgment
- Rationalization
- Self-pity
- Unresolved grief
- Persistent unrealistic worry
- Feelings of worthlessness
- Drug-oriented lifestyle
- Situational factors leading to relapse
- Intense unexpressed feelings

This is a crucial decision point in treatment. Not all problems in this category require care in an inpatient environment. Most staff interventions would be more appropriate in a lower level of care.

Really, the only things holding the patient in the hospital at this point are discharge screens, which will be addressed later in this chapter.

EXAMPLES OF STAFF INTERVENTIONS

- 1:1 therapies
- Behavioral contracts
- Education about treatment
- Group, psychotherapy, and other talk therapies
- Leisure skills groups
- Milieu management
- Peer pressure/support
- Confrontation

2–1 Point Five—Educate

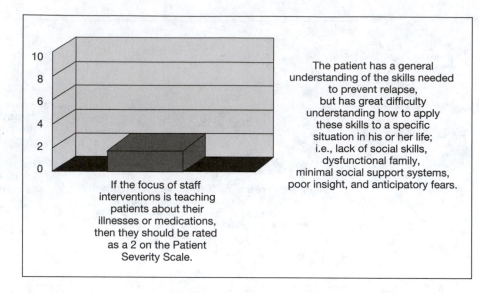

The patient has a general understanding of the skills needed to prevent relapse, but has great difficulty understanding how to apply these skills to a specific situation in his or her life; i.e., lack of social skills, dysfunctional family, minimal social support systems, poor insight, and anticipatory fears.

If the focus of staff interventions is teaching patients about their illnesses or medications, then they should be rated as a 2 on the Patient Severity Scale.

EXAMPLES OF POSSIBLE PROBLEM STATEMENTS

- Academic deficit
- Academic and work performance difficulty
- Blaming others
- Codependency
- Defines substance abuse excluding self
- Difficulty structuring free time without chemical use
- Disturbed communication skills
- Drug-oriented lifestyle
- Dysfunctional pattern of communication
- Fear related to a specific situation
- History of a main relationship with another individual active in chemical dependency
- Inability to control chemical intake/illness
- Lack of understanding regarding illness
- Primary social group uses drugs
- Projection of blame/responsibility
- Reading/writing difficulties
- No occupational/vocational skills
- Impaired job functioning due to substance abuse/illness

Patient at this level have minimal need for hospitalization. With rare exceptions, these patients can be moved to the next level of the continuum of care. Only discharge screens would keep these patients in an inpatient setting. If the treatment team decides to keep these patients in an inpatient setting, they should carefully document the reasons why they believe this problem continues to be a blockage to discharge.

EXAMPLES OF STAFF INTERVENTIONS

- 1:1 therapies
- Behavioral contracts
- Education about treatment
- Group, psychotherapy, and other talk therapies
- Leisure skills groups
- Milieu management
- Peer pressure/support
- Confrontation
- Journals/listing (experiences, triggers to behaviors)
- Role playing
- Vocational/occupational/ leisure skill assessments and training
- Social skills retraining
- Family therapy

0–Point six—Reintegration

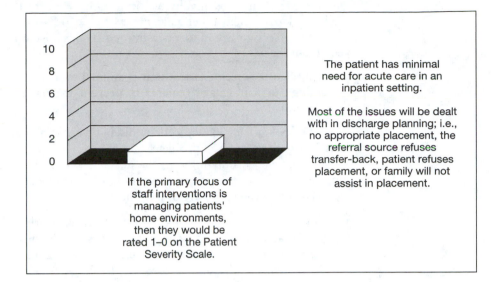

The patient has minimal need for acute care in an inpatient setting.

Most of the issues will be dealt with in discharge planning; i.e., no appropriate placement, the referral source refuses transfer-back, patient refuses placement, or family will not assist in placement.

If the primary focus of staff interventions is managing patients' home environments, then they would be rated 1–0 on the Patient Severity Scale.

EXAMPLES OF POSSIBLE PROBLEM STATEMENTS:

- Difficulty structuring free time without chemical use
- Disturbed communication skill
- Disturbed relationship
- Drug-oriented lifestyle
- History of a main relationship with another individual active in chemical dependency
- Primary social group uses drugs
- Projection of blame/ responsibility
- Legal difficulties
- Marital discord
- Unaware of relapse issues
- Environmental issues
- No occupational/vocational skills
- Financial issues
- Transportation issues

EXAMPLES OF STAFF INTERVENTIONS

- Educational/vocational assessments
- Behavioral contracts
- Education about community resources
- Medical/therapeutic follow-up/ referral
- Referral to partial day/ outpatient treatment
- Housing referrals
- Long-term treatment referral
- Education regarding necessary medical testing/follow-up
- Family meetings
- Arrangement for caregiver
- Caregiver education
- Financial counseling/follow-up
- Arranging for outpatient medication

Discharge Screens

Discharge screens are invaluable in deciding when the patient can be discharged from his or her current level of care. Although it is true that intensity of service gets patients admitted to the hospital, discharge screens keep them there!

A discharge screen is a test that is applied to a specific problem to see if enough of a blockage remains to prevent the patient from leaving the hospital.

Let's look at an example of a discharge screen that is a blockage to discharge for this medical problem.

The patient was admitted to the hospital with a dangerously high blood sugar level. The possibility of harm was imminent. Here is how the patient moved through the hierarchy of treatment.

- Protect—The patient was admitted and hourly blood tests were immediately instituted. The patient was given injections of insulin in regulated amounts until the blood sugar was significantly decreased and the patient's condition was downgraded.
- Stable—Although the patient's condition was now stable, he or she had no desire to manage blood sugar levels. Therapeutic steps were instituted to give the patient insight into the need for acceptable diabetes management.
- Direct—The nursing staff outlined a plan of action to manage the patient's diabetes and after a dietary consult the patient was put on a diabetic diet and a regular course of insulin therapy.
- Educate—Nursing and medical staff taught the patient how to measure blood sugar, administer insulin, select dosage, and the methods of administration.

At this point in treatment, the patient is fully capable of taking care of his own diabetes. However, one problem remains that prevents the patient from being discharged to home. Before he or she can be discharged, the patient must have insulin and syringes at home. Although the current level of inpatient care would not be severe enough to warrant admission to the hospital (intensity of care), until the patient has medication at home he or she cannot be reintegrated into the next level of care (discharge blockage).

Other types of blockages may include, but are not limited to, the following:

- Educational/vocational assessments
- Education about community resources
- Medical/therapeutic follow-up/referral
- Referral to partial day/outpatient treatment
- Housing referrals
- Long-term treatment referral
- Education regarding necessary medical testing/follow-up
- Family meetings
- Arrangement for a caregiver
- Caregiver education
- Financial counseling/follow-up
- Durable medical equipment

Now that we have outlined a universally applicable scale for measuring acuity, Chapter 13 will examine see how the same scale can be adapted to measure outcomes.

CHAPTER 12 SELF-TEST

Answer the following questions. When you have completed the test, check your answers in Appendix B.

1. What is an acuity scale?

2. What is the primary disadvantage to rating patient progress using subjective ordinate scales?

3. What are the six stages of recovery?

4. What is a discharge screen?

5. At what point on the Patient Severity Scale should the team begin to monitor the continued use of inpatient treatment?

There are three kinds of lies—lies, damned lies, and statistics. — **Mark Twain**

Statistics are like a bikini. What they reveal is suggestive, but what they conceal is vital. — **Aaron Levenstein**

Measuring Outcomes

13

THE TRUTH IS RELATIVE

For years, the treatment providers and insurance communities have discussed outcomes. Yet there is still no universally accepted measurement of patient outcomes. Why? Because outcomes mean accountability and a great deal of behavioral health treatment cannot withstand the scrutiny.

Even more than this, the term "successful outcome" means different things to different people. Success is relative; in fact, truth is relative! What people perceive to be a fact, *is* indeed fact to them. Additionally, what is truth to one is a lie to another. To clear up some of this confusion as it relates to treatment, let's look as some common expectations regarding behavioral health treatment in general.

Perception of Treatment Is Reality

There can be no doubt that people look at issues differently. Just because they are looking at the same issue, does not mean they see the same thing. Here is a perfect example:

> **If two people were standing opposite of each other and reading the same magazine, would they both see the same thing?**

No, one would see the front of the magazine and the other would see the back. Same magazine, but each viewer would see a different view of the *exact same object*. Whose view is the true picture? In fact, both see the truth! They just see it from their own perspective.

Healthcare Perspectives

Here are some common perceptions of health care from different viewpoints.

- Providers feel like they do not have adequate time to treat their patients.
- Patients feel like they should get more treatment for their money (insurance payments and accessibility).
- Insurance companies feel like they pay for unnecessary, unsubstantiated treatment.

From the provider standpoint, the lengths of stay have been shortened, so the insurance companies can make more money. From the insurance companies' standpoint, they protect themselves against the providers padding their pockets by overutilizing care.

From the patients' perspective, they pay a major portion of their check for insurance coverage and they do not feel like they get enough care for their money. The truth is, they do pay a major premium for their insurance, but from the insurance company's point of view, even if you added up a year's worth of premiums it would not cover two days in a hospital. Can there be a common ground?

John D. Cone, Ph.D. (*Evaluating Outcomes: Empirical Tools for Effective Practice*. Washington, DC: American Psychological Association) says there are six reasons to measure outcomes.

1. To satisfy our intellectual curiosity
2. To provide economic and financial information
3. To provide practice efficiency
4. To maintain increased ethical standards
5. To avoid errors in judgment
6. To obtain information not available in published literature

Although these reasons make a lot of sense, the issue of outcomes measurement is critical for gauging diagnostic success; to do that, everyone has to be on the same page.

How do we measure treatment success or outcomes? Before we can measure treatment outcomes or physician and patient satisfaction, we must have a universal language. If everyone has a different definition of treatment success based on different criteria, it is difficult to agree on common ground. Unfortunately, outcomes measurement has been elusive for the following reasons:

1. Everyone has a different expectation of treatment success.
2. Accountability is scary.
3. Patients with different diagnoses look and act differently.

If all this sounds familiar, it is because many of these same issues were discussed in the previous chapter.

*   To have a universal outcomes measurement, all parties need a universal measurement unit.
*   To begin with, all parties would have to agree that treatment is an ongoing process and success can be measured by the progress a patient makes and not just by curative results.
*   To have a universal outcomes measurement, there would have to be agreement that treatment is a process that encompasses many levels of the continuum of care.
*   Finally, these outcome scales would have to be based on the focus of staff interventions and the intensity of the problems being treated, not a target symptomology.

At the beginning of this chapter, Mark Twain is quoted as having said, "There are three kinds of lies—lies, damned lies, and statistics." This statement proves a point: Without universal measurement criteria, anyone can manipulate treatment data toward a favorable end.

Let's look at an example of this very problem. During the early days of alcoholism treatment, treatment teams used to quote phenomenal treatment success statistics. Some programs even touted that 90% of patients had positive treatment outcomes. The key to this phrase is what constituted a "treatment success." After closer study, a success in this case was defined as, "no interaction with the legal systems." These patients could be drinking or using drugs every night, but if they did not get in legal trouble because of their using or drinking, they were considered a treatment success.

Was this truly a treatment success story? Well, if you accept the narrowly defined interpretation, yes. In addition, if the insurers and potential patients did not know the measurement of success, they would naturally assume that 90% of the patients treated in this particular treatment program remained sober. Did 90% remain sober? No, of course they did not.

Again, is sobriety alone an accurate measurement of treatment success? Isn't the goal of alcoholism treatment—sobriety? Well, yes and no. Is it a treatment success to have a "dry drunk"; that is, an alcoholic who has quit drinking but is miserable and making anyone they come in contact with just as miserable? No! The patient is sober but hardly a treatment success.

Now, what if a position on the treatment continuum was used to define recovery and outcome? The alcoholic who stops drinking no longer needs the medical protection of a detox environment. He or she has enough motivation to want to begin sobriety, but not enough tools to manage his or her life at this point in recovery. If all parties understood where the patient was on the hierarchy of treatment intensity, then they would have a universal gauge of the progress made thus far in treatment.

Using the hierarchy of treatment intensity to measure outcomes is not just a simple process of measuring where the patient fits in the hierarchy; in fact, that would be just a start. Let's look at the structure of the hierarchy as it relates to the patient severity scales (see Figure 13.1).

The higher the priority and intensity of treatment, the higher it must be prioritized in the treatment process and the quicker it must be carried out. In fact, protecting will always be the first thing a treatment team does for any patient. How do we know this? It's simple—you cannot treat a dead patient!

The entire hierarchy is inversely related to the recovery treatment process. That is to say, the higher the patient's acuity, the faster the staff will focus on that particular need and the quicker that focus of treatment is prioritized. Therefore, the scale is inverted. The first level of treatment, *protecting and stabilizing,* is the highest level of priority on the hierarchy. Motivating the patient is the second treatment task in an inverted scale throughout the hierarchy.

Take a look at Figure 13.2. In this example, we have combined Protect and Stabilize and they have become the first scheduled treatment tasks for our scales. After the patient is stabilized, the team changes the focus of his or her treatment to tackle the next level of need, and so on, until the patient is moved forward in the continuum of care.

Figure 13.1 | Hierarchy structure in relation to Patient Severity Scales

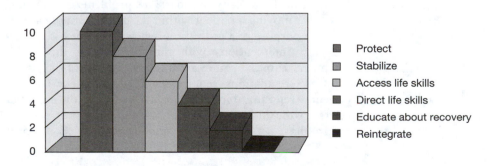

Figure 13.2 | Hierarchy of treatment intensity in relation to acuity and task priority

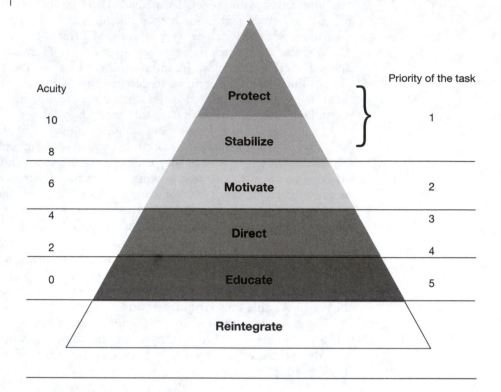

Unfortunately, it is not always this simple; in reality, this process only explains the first element in an outcome scale. The treatment team can pinpoint the focus of the treatment team's level of intervention in the recovery process and by doing so, measure patient acuity and the severity of the problem. Still, this is only part of the picture. The treatment team understands how far the patient has come in treatment. But how will the treatment team know if the patient can be safely moved to a different level of care? In order to accomplish this task, the therapist must add another point of view to the hierarchy of care.

The Utilization Review Grid

To have a full understanding of the patient's position on the outcome scale, the staff has to match the intensity of the treatment interventions with the type of problem they are treating and any pertinent discharge screens. The treatment team can accomplish this by using a utilization review grid. Remember, the severity of a patient's problems cannot be the single deciding factor for moving a patient within the continuum of care.

The purpose of a utilization review grid index is to match the intensity of the staff interventions with the intensity of the problem to allow the treatment team to acquire a full representation of the patient's problem.

CMS regulations require that the treatment team address all of the patient's relevant, biopsychosocial problems during treatment. This term refers to the holistic nature of the patient's problems. Not only does the patient have to deal with several different types of problems (biological, psychological, and social), but each of these problems has a different level of intensity. Let's begin by looking at the term *biopsychosocial* and refine the types of problems it describes.

1. *Biological* = Medical or physiological problems. These issues are physical or chemical in nature and constitute the highest degree of severity.
2. *Psychological* = Problems with personality, feelings, thoughts or intellect.
3. *Sociological* = Environmental and social problems to include: family, drug-related lifestyles, employment, and can the patient safely return to this environment.

Each of these problems represents a decrease in intensity. Medical problems have a higher severity than environmental problems. In order to create a complete picture of our patient's status, the treatment team must consider both the type of problem and the intensity of the treatment modalities necessary to manage the problem.

Think of the grid as a roadmap. Visualize a map and the distance grid or legend. To use the grid, you would pick the city you are departing from and the one you are going to. Where the points intersect on the grid is the distance between the two points.

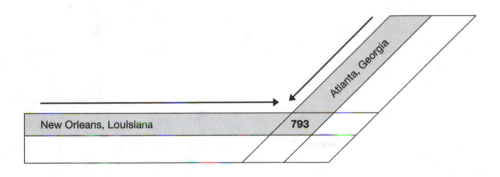

The utilization review grid works in the same way. Across the top of the grid are the three types of problems: medical, relationships, and environment. The guide numbers across the top of the grid indicate the severity of the type of problem and the order in which the problems are addressed.

	1	2	3
	Medical	Relationships	Environmental
1	1	2	3

The numbers going down the grid represent the order of priority the staff will use to address each segment of the acuity scale. Protect and stabilize is first.

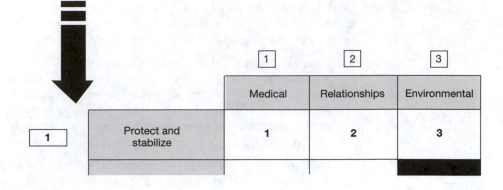

Now the team can begin to read and use the grid to make decisions about moving the patient through the continuum of care.

Simply pick the type of problem and the focus of staff interventions and follow the line to get a utilization review grid score!

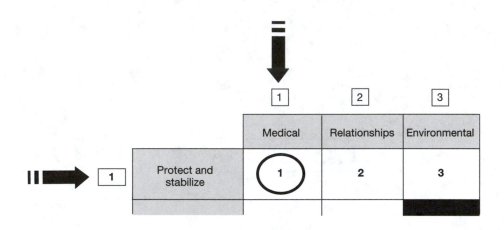

Additionally, we have a complete, graphic representation of exactly where the patient is in treatment. Anyone who looks at the grid can instantaneously tell what the staff is doing for the patient and what types of problems the staff is dealing with.

Scoring the Grid

All problems with a grid score of five and under indicate a need for hospitalization or continued care in an inpatient environment unless a discharge screen prevents a change in the treatment environment. Realistically (in today's reimbursement environment) the team should start making plans to move the patient into another point on the continuum at about level four.

In the most recent example, the grid tells the team that they are treating a medical problem that requires the patient to be protected or stabilized. The grid scores this combination (protect + medical) or $(1 \times 1 = 1)$ as the highest priority of need for inpatient treatment.

Here is another scoring example.

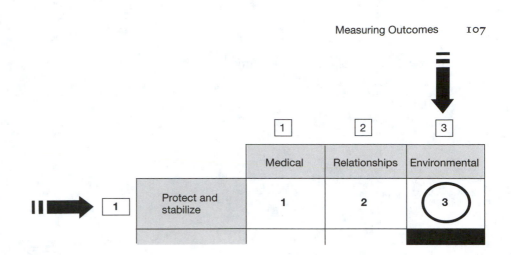

The need to protect a patient from abusive relationships or a dangerous environment has a lower severity factor than protecting a patient in medical distress. The problem is still *very* severe, but environmental problems alone are not severe enough to keep a patient in a hospital. That is, unless the patient would be harmed by returning them to that environment. Matching the components of the grid (protect + environment) or (1 × 3 = 3) still indicates the need for possible inpatient treatment because the grid score is less than five. *Remember that the client can be moved to another point of care on the continuum as soon as arrangements have been made.*

Remember, the problem severity is not the only indication that patients need inpatient treatment.

Discharge screens would indicate that you cannot send a patient home, if there is a reasonable certainty that the patient would be injured in that environment. In other words, the problems severity alone does not indicate a continued need for inpatient treatment but the discharge screen prevents the staff from returning a patient to a dangerous environment. There are many good alternatives on the continuum of care for patients who cannot return home (e.g., group homes, residential care, foster homes, etc.), and a treatment team must plan for an alternative living environment before the patient can be discharged.

The Utilization Review Grid Score

Utilization review is a term that refers to insurance companies managing the utilization (usage) of the different types of care provided for their patients. Obviously the insurance companies want to see that their patients are treated in the *least* restrictive environment, both because it costs less and, in many cases, is therapeutically advantageous. The purpose of the utilization review grid score is to give the patients, staff, and insurance companies a common language (see Figure 13.3). As previously discussed, using a common point of reference is the key to outcome studies and utilization review.

The treatment team can now use this scale as a reference for patient progress. The team can plot an exact combination of factors and pinpoint the patient's progress, or lack of progress, at any point on the continuum of care.

When the staff or therapist uses the utilization review grid scores as a measurement of patient progress, they can pinpoint all of the following factors using a universally accepted measurement.

Figure 13.3 | Utilization review grid index

	1	2	3
	Medical	Relationships	Environmental
1 Protect and stabilize	1	2	3
2 Motivate patient to want treatment	2	4	6
3 Direct treatment	3	6	9
4 Educate about recovery	4	8	12
5 Reintegrate into the community	5	10	15

1. What type of problem the treatment team is treating.
2. What the focus of therapeutic intervention is.
3. What the patient's progress in treatment is.
4. What the point in treatment is when the patient should be moved forward in the continuum of care.

CHAPTER 13 SELF-TEST

Answer the following questions. When you have completed the test, check your answers in Appendix B.

1. What does "perception is reality" mean?

2. What are three reasons that outcomes measurement has been elusive?

3. What is the purpose of a utilization review grid?

4. What is meant by the term *biopsychosocial*?

5. What are the staff tasks (focii) of treatment in the order that the patient receives them?

Treatment Planning Practicum

## 14

Garbage in . . . garbage out.

TRANSFERRING KNOWLEDGE TO FORM

Treatment planning is much more than knowing what forms to use or what they should look like. Almost everyone has heard the phrase "garbage in . . . garbage out" regarding computers. The treatment planning process is no different. Good treatment planning requires a transfer of knowledge and information from the assessment tools to the planning and implementation phase of treatment.

Forms help the treatment team present an ordered, logical picture of treatment in a legible format. However, if the team is just filling out the forms to meet federal and state guidelines, what they produce is just clinical garbage.

Here is a basic example of a typical clinical history. In this exercise the student will find the pertinent clinical information and transfer it onto treatment planning forms. The objective is to plan effective mental health treatment.

MOCK CLINICAL HISTORY #1

Name: William F. Landry
DOB: 8/14/1936
Religion: Roman Catholic

Reason for Admission

This 64-year-old, married, currently unemployed, Caucasian male was admitted to City Hospital for treatment of depression. Mr. Landry presented himself to the emergency room after an overdose of Prozac in a suicide attempt. Mr. Landry stated, "I've got nothing to live for and I just want to die." After having his stomach pumped, Mr. Landry was stabilized medically, and referred for admission to the psychiatric service. The patient's admission status was voluntary.

This information was collected from the patient and his wife, and verified with his daughter, Joyce. The information is considered reliable.

Admission Criteria

1. The patient is a danger to himself.
2. The patient attempted suicide within the last 8 hours.
3. The patient is unable to attend to activities of daily living.

Chief Complaint

Mr. Landry feels that he has become useless because of his forced retirement. He feels that he has nothing to live for, and he wants to die.

Presenting Problems

The patient presents with a current history of suicidal behavior and depressive mood disturbance. Three months ago, the patient was forced to accept an early mandatory retirement from his job with Regal Paper Company. Since that time Mr. Landry has become increasingly withdrawn and sullen. He spends days in his room with the blinds drawn and lying in bed. He sleeps continuously and has trouble getting out of bed. He states, "I just don't have the energy to do anything." At the present time, Mr. Landry is medically stable and has no physical complaints.

Review of Systems

The patient does not currently exhibit physical complaints and is taking 20 mg of Prozac B.I.D. (twice a day) and a combination of multivitamins. The patient has not verbalized any physical complaints and the H&P is negative for any serious medical or surgical problems.

Past Medical History

The patient states that he has had a history of malaria, which was contracted in the Philippines while in the service. He has never been admitted to any facility for mental disturbances or alcohol or drug abuse, but is currently under the care of a psychologist for outpatient treatment of depression as part of his retirement outplacement package.

Family History

Mr. Landry is the third of five siblings. There are two older sisters and two younger brothers. All of his siblings are living but both parents are deceased. The family has no history of alcohol or drug abuse or psychiatric illness.

Social Interaction

The patient is married. He has two children, a 40-year-old son and a 38-year-old daughter. Mr. Landry has a college degree, and had worked as an engineer for Regal Paper Company since 1960. He is currently retired and lives with his wife, Karen.

Mr. and Mrs. Landry have been married for more than 40 years. Mrs. Landry is currently working as a medical technologist at a local hospital. They are both members of St. Rita's Catholic Church.

Mr. Landry's sexual preference is heterosexual, and he has no current, pending legal charges.

Mental Status Examination

Appearance
This 64-year-old, Caucasian male appears somewhat older than his stated age. He is nicely dressed and is neat and clean.

Consciousness
Mr. Landry appears sleepy, which is probably an effect of the current medications.

Orientation
The patient is fully oriented to person, time, and place.

Behavior
Mr. Landry is somewhat agitated. He seems embarrassed by his situation and slumped in his chair during our interview.

Attitude
The patient's attitude is cooperative.

Affect
The patient's affect seems somewhat blunted and flat and he seems particularly withdrawn, tired, and sad. His vocabulary seems stunted and he seems to be moving in slow motion. Mr. Landry is displaying a very narrow range of affect.

Mood
Mr. Landry describes himself as very sad and tired. He states, "My depression has been much worse for the last 24 hours." The patient seems disinterested in positive news.

Energy
The patient has a very low energy level, and currently seems somewhat disorganized.

Speech
The patient is using a very flat, monotone voice.

Thinking Process
The patient is not delusional but does seem to be obsessing on his forced retirement and thoughts of suicide. Mr. Landry was admitted to the psychiatric service after his stomach was pumped out in the ER. He remains a suicide risk, but is not a risk to others nor is he aggressive.

Perception
The patient is not experiencing any auditory, visual, or tactile hallucinations.

Medically Unexplained Somatic Symptoms

There are none and the patient denies ever assuming another personality.

Paroxysmal Attacks

Patient denies any symptoms.

Memory

The patient's short term and remote memory seems intact.

Attention and Concentration

The patient seems easily distracted and has trouble with serial 3s.

Intelligence and Knowledge

The patient is of above-normal intelligence and is a college graduate. He understands abstract concepts and seems to be functioning at an above-average level.

Insight

The patient has insight into his problems, in that he is able to relate the symptoms of his depression to the loss of his job.

Judgment

At the current time the patient is exhibiting very poor judgment and is still considered a danger to himself.

Additional Information

1. Estimated length of stay is five to seven days.
2. Mr. Landry will have to be encouraged and motivated to participate in the treatment milieu.

Discharge Criteria

1. Absence of any suicidal ideation.
2. Able to verbalize a realistic plan for the future.
3. Able to verbalize significant relapse factors.

Preliminary Treatment Plan

1. Protect until stable.
2. Increase his insight into his anger and how that relates to his suicide attempt.
3. Plan activities for postdischarge.

Admission Diagnoses:

Axis I: Major Depressive Disorder, Single Episode, Severe

Axis II: None

Axis III: History of Malaria

Axis IV: Problems relating to Social Environment (Mr. Landry has been forced to retire and feels used and useless.)

Axis V: Current 10; Past Year 67

Recommendations for Treatment

1. Decrease suicidal ideation
2. Decrease depressive symptomology
3. Decrease agitation

Treatment Modalities to Be Used

1. Group and individual therapy
3. OT/RT
3. Nursing education

4. Leisure skills planning
5. Psychological testing
6. Medication management

Maintain Patient Safety

1. Suicidal Precautions
2. Close Observation Q15 (every 15 minutes)

Initial Post-discharge Information
1. Return to home
2. Follow-up with Dr. Gad at the Mental Health Center
3. Involvement with RSVP
4. Medical follow-up with family physician

The patient has no physical disabilities or language restrictions and is able to read and write.

This clinical history will serve as the basis for the student to develop a treatment plan. Usually there are more assessments to consider. For the purposes of this exercise, this one clinical history will suffice.

EXERCISE: DEVELOPING A TREATMENT PLAN

In this exercise, the student will go through the process of developing a plan of care for Mr. Landry. The student will use all of the suggested forms and extrapolate the information from the clinical history. Additionally, the student should develop the plan of care using *The Rule of Four Ps*. This simple format allows the student to manage the clinical information in an orderly manner and is an excellent tool for developing a plan of care.

THE RULE OF FOUR Ps
✓ **Peruse** the completed clinical information and assessments.
✓ **Pick** out the problems that block the patient's discharge to the next level of care.
✓ **Prioritize** the importance of the problems to be treated. Only treat discharge blockages.
✓ **Plan** a realistic problem resolution for the patient.

Peruse the completed clinical information and assessments. Begin by reviewing the clinical history in detail. Use a highlighter to indicate problems that have been identified. Review the clinician's recommendations for treatment and begin thinking how they can be used as interventions.

Pick out the problems that block the patient's discharge to the next level of care.

List five problems that were identified in the clinical history.

1.

2.

3.

4.

5.

Prioritize the importance of the problems to be treated. Treat only discharge blockages.

Now, take the same five problems identified in the clinical history and rearrange them based on the focus of treatment and the intensity of the problem.

1.

2.

3.

4.

5.

Plan a realistic problem resolution for the patient. After the student has completed the first four tasks, he or she is ready to develop a treatment plan. Using the blank forms that follow, please transfer your clinical decisions and problems into a complete treatment plan. Use the student's name as the case manager.

Using the blank forms that follow (Figure 14.1 to 14.8) write a problem resolution plan on only the first problem on the priority list. You will not fill out a treatment team update sheet. When you have completed the treatment plan, compare it to the example plan that follows in this workbook (Figures 14.9 to 14.16).

Figure 14.1 | Master Treatment Plan Cover Sheet

Addressograph Imprint	Master Treatment Plan Cover Sheet

Case Manager	Nurse	Age	Marital Status

Legal Status	Date Master Plan Opened	Estimated LOS	Ethnic Background

CRITERIA FOR ADMISSION

☐ Suicidal Ideation
☐ Suicide Plan with an Instrument
☐ Suicide Attempt or Gesture
☐ Danger to Self
☐ Danger to Others
☐ Unable to Carry out Activities of Daily Living
☐ Actively Psychotic
☐ Medical Detoxification
☐ Failure of Outpatient Treatment
☐ Active Sexual or Physical Abuse (C&A)
☐ Comprehensive Medical or Psychiatric Evaluation
☐ Medication Adjustment that must be done in a Hospital

SAFETY / RISK ANALYSIS ISSUES ON ADMISSION

Precautions for these Problem Behaviors

The Patient is on the following Unit Restrictions

The Patient is on the following Medical Protocols

INITIAL DISCHARGE PLAN

Post Discharge Living Arrangements	Physician Follow-up	Active Legal Issues Affecting Treatment

Physical Handicaps or Limitations	Dietary Problems / Special Diet	Language Barriers

Can the Patient Read?   ☐ YES   ☐ NO   Can the Patient Write?   ☐ YES   ☐ NO

Notes: _____

Figure 14.2 | Assessment of Strengths and Weaknesses

Addressograph Imprint	**Assessment of Strengths and Weaknesses**

5 4 3 2 1

☐ ☐ ☐ ☐ ☐ Capable of independent Living

_____

☐ ☐ ☐ ☐ ☐ Insight / Judgment

_____

☐ ☐ ☐ ☐ ☐ Good Physical Abilities / Health

_____

☐ ☐ ☐ ☐ ☐ Ability to Stand up for Rights

_____

☐ ☐ ☐ ☐ ☐ Community Support Network

_____

☐ ☐ ☐ ☐ ☐ Employment

_____

☐ ☐ ☐ ☐ ☐ Ability to express feelings

_____

☐ ☐ ☐ ☐ ☐ Motivated for Treatment

_____

☐ ☐ ☐ ☐ ☐ Positive Marriage

_____

☐ ☐ ☐ ☐ ☐ Intelligence

_____

☐ ☐ ☐ ☐ ☐ Vocational / Occupational Skills

_____

☐ ☐ ☐ ☐ ☐ Education

_____

☐ ☐ ☐ ☐ ☐ Leisure Skills and Interests

_____

5=EXCELLENT   4=GOOD   3=AVERAGE   2=FAIR   1= POOR

Figure 14.3 | Axis I, II & III Diagnosis Sheet

	Axis I, II & III Diagnosis Sheet
Addressograph Imprint	

AXIS I DIAGNOSIS

	C	D	M	R
_____	C	D	M	R
_____	C	D	M	R
_____	C	D	M	R
_____	C	D	M	R
_____	C	D	M	R
_____	C	D	M	R
_____	C	D	M	R
_____	C	D	M	R

AXIS II DIAGNOSIS

	C	D	M	R
_____	C	D	M	R
_____	C	D	M	R
_____	C	D	M	R

AXIS III DIAGNOSIS

	C	D	M	R
_____	C	D	M	R
_____	C	D	M	R
_____	C	D	M	R
_____	C	D	M	R
_____	C	D	M	R
_____	C	D	M	R
_____	C	D	M	R
_____	C	D	M	R

DIAGNOSIS CODES

C	This diagnosis is **COMPLETED**. The patient has achieved closure and the desired therapeutic results have been achieved
D	This diagnosis is **DEFERRED**. Although the problem requires care, it does not need to be actively treated at this time
M	This diagnosis is an existing problem with an existing plan of care which we will **MAINTAIN**
R	This diagnosis has been identified for treatment, however the patient has **REFUSED** treatment

Figure 14.4 | Axis IV Psychosocial Stressors

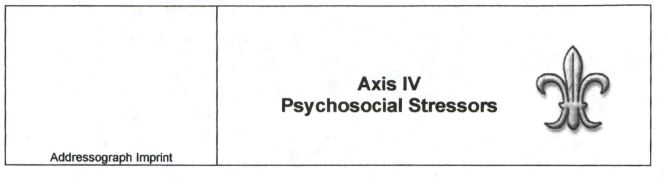

Axis IV Psychosocial Stressors

Addressograph Imprint

Problem with Primary Support Group:_____

_____

Death of family member, health problems in family disruption of family by separation; divorce or estrangement; removal from the home; remarriage
of a parent; sexual or physical abuse parental over-protection neglect of a child;- inadequate discipline, discord with siblings; birth of a sibling.

Problem Relating to the Social Environment:_____

_____

Death or loss of a friend, inadequate social support, living alone; difficulty with acculturation discrimination; adjustment to lifestyle transition (such a retirement

Educational Problems:_____

_____

Illiteracy; academic problems-, discord with teachers or classmate inadequate school or environment

Occupational Problems:_____

_____

Unemployment threat of job loss; difficult work schedule, difficult work conditions; job change discord with boss or co-workers.

Housing Problems:_____

_____

hopelessness; inadequate housing; unsafe neighborhood; discord with neighbors or landlord

Economic Problems:_____

_____

Extreme poverty inadequate finances insufficient welfare support

Problems with Access to Health Care Services:_____

_____

inadequate health care services; transportation to health care facilities unavailable, inadequate health care insurance

Problems Related to Interaction with the Legal System/Crime:_____

_____

arrest; incarceration; litigation; victim of crime

Other Psychological and Environmental Problems: _____

_____

Exposure to disease, war, other hostilities; discord with non-family care giver such as counselors, social workers or physicians, unavailability of social agencies

Figure 14.5 | Axis V GAF Scale

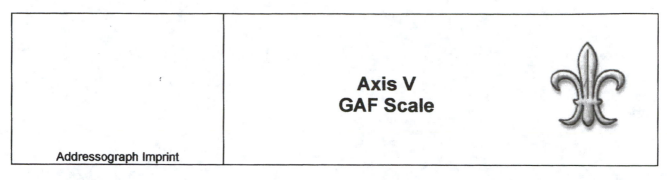

	Axis V GAF Scale	
Addressograph Imprint		

100-91

– Superior functioning in a wide range of activities, life's problems never seem to get out of hand, is sought out by others because of his or her many positive qualities. No symptoms-

90-81

– Absent or minimal symptoms (e.g., mild anxiety before an exam), good functioning in all areas, interested and involved in a wide range of activities, socially effective, generally satisfied with life, no more than everyday problems or concerns (e.g.., an occasional argument with family members).

80-71

– If symptoms are present, they are transient and expectable reactions to psychosocial stressors (e.g., difficulty concentrating after family y argument) no more than slight impairment in social, occupational, Or school functioning (e.g., temporarily falling behind in schoolwork).

70-61

– Some Mild symptoms (e.g., depressed mood and mild insomnia) OR some difficulty in social, occupational, or school functioning (e.g., occasional truancy, or theft within the household), but generally functioning pretty well, has some meaningful interpersonal relationships

60-51

– Moderate symptoms (e.g., flat effect and circumstantial speech, occasional panic attacks, OR moderate difficulty in social, occupational, or school functioning (e.g., few friends, unable to keep a job).

50-41

– Serious symptoms (e.g., suicidal ideation, severe obsessional rituals, frequent shoplifting) OR any serious impairment in social, occupational, or school functioning, (e.g., no friends, unable to keep a job).

40-31

– Some impairment in reality testing or communication (e.g., speech is at times illogical, obscure, or irrelevant), OR major impairment in several areas, such as work or school, family relations, judgment, thinking or mood (e-g-, depressed man avoids friends, neglects family, and is unable to work, child frequently beats up younger children, is defiant at home, and is failing at school).

30-21

– Behavior is considerably influenced by delusions or hallucinations OR serious impairment In communication or judgment (e.g., sometimes incoherent, acts grossly inappropriately, suicidal preoccupation) OR inability to function in almost all areas (e.g., stays in bed all day, no job, home, friends).

20-11

– Some danger of hurting self or others (e.g., suicide attempts without dear expectation of death, frequently violent; manic excitement OR occasionally fails; to maintain minimal personal hygiene (e.g., smears feces) OR gross impairment in communication (e.g., largely incoherent or mute).

10-1

– Persistent danger of severely hurting self Or Others (recurrent violence) OR persistent inability to maintain minimal Personal hygiene OR serious suicidal act with clears expectation of death.

0

– Inadequate information

GAF Score Prior Year	GAF Score on Admission	GAF Score on Discharge

Source: Reprinted with permission from the *Diagnostic and Statistical Manual of Mental Disorders*, Fourth Edition, Text Revision. Copyright © 2000 American Psychiatric Association.

Figure 14.6 | Master Treatment Plan Problem List

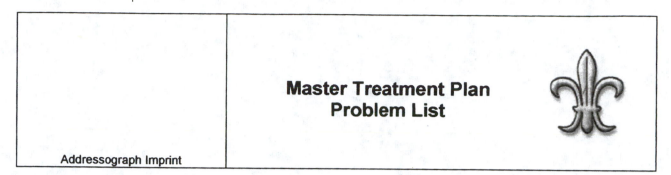

	Master Treatment Plan Problem List	
Addressograph Imprint		

AXIS I&II (Psychiatric, Psychological and Problems with Mental Retardation

Date Opened	Problem #	Problem Description	Problem Status	Date Changed
___/___/___	_____	_____	C D M R	___/___/___
___/___/___	_____	_____	C D M R	___/___/___
___/___/___	_____	_____	C D M R	___/___/___
___/___/___	_____	_____	C D M R	___/___/___
___/___/___	_____	_____	C D M R	___/___/___
___/___/___	_____	_____	C D M R	___/___/___
___/___/___	_____	_____	C D M R	___/___/___
___/___/___	_____	_____	C D M R	___/___/___

AXIS III (Medical Problems)*

*Remember all Axis III diagnosis must be opened as problem statements

Date Changed

Date Opened	Problem #	Problem Description	Problem Status	Date Changed
___/___/___	_____	_____	C D M R	___/___/___
___/___/___	_____	_____	C D M R	___/___/___
___/___/___	_____	_____	C D M R	___/___/___
___/___/___	_____	_____	C D M R	___/___/___
___/___/___	_____	_____	C D M R	___/___/___
___/___/___	_____	_____	C D M R	___/___/___
___/___/___	_____	_____	C D M R	___/___/___
___/___/___	_____	_____	C D M R	___/___/___
___/___/___	_____	_____	C D M R	___/___/___

PROBLEM CODES

C	This problem is COMPLETED. The patient has achieved closure and the desired therapeutic results have been achieved
D	This problem is DEFERRED. although the problem requires care, it does not need to be actively treated at this time
M	This problem is an existing problem with an existing plan of care which we will MAINTAIN
R	This problem has been identified for treatment, however the patient has REFUSED treatment

Figure 14.7 | Problem Resolution Plan

Problem Resolution Plan

Addressograph Imprint

PROBLEM #	PROBLEM STATEMENT	DATE OPENED

MANIFESTATIONS OF THE PROBLEM
What behaviors describes the problem?

_____

_____

_____

_____

LONG TERM GOAL
How can the patient demonstrate that they can be safely discharged?

LTG #		TARGET DATE
	_____	
	_____	

SHORT TERM GOAL
What intermediate step will be used to measure progress toward discharge goal?

STG #		TARGET DATE
	_____	
	_____	

#	INTERVENTIONS

List who is responsible for this intervention by name and discipline	List the modality, milieu or treatment group used to do the intervention	Describe the focus of the intervention and the expected result of participation	List the frequency of the intervention

Figure 14.8 | Treatment Team / Patient Signature Sheet

Treatment Team / Patient Signature Sheet

Addressograph Imprint

☐ Initial Planning Session ☐ Initial Treatment Team ☐ Planning Update ☐ Administrative

The Following Team Members Participated in the Interdisciplinary Treatment Plans, Reviews or Updates

Attending Physician: _____

Case Manager: _____

Social Worker: _____

Psychologist: _____

Activity Therapy: _____

Nursing: _____

_____

Other Allied Professional: _____

_____

_____

_____

ATTENTION

PATIENT / FAMILY INVOLVEMENT

This plan has been explained to the patient or appropriate other person.
The patient or other appropriate person has been give the opportunity to ask questions and participate in the plan for their care as documented below.

My signature attests to my participation in treatment planning and correctly documents my level of participation

☐ Contributed to Goals and Plan ☐ Present at Team Meeting ☐ Unable to Participate
☐ Aware of Plan and Contract ☐ Refused to Participate ☐ Refused to Sign Plan

Patient Signature _____ Date_____/_____/_____

Family Member's Signature _____ Date_____/_____/_____

CHECK YOUR WORK: FINDING PROBLEMS

Let's see how you did. You should have begun your plan by reviewing the clinical history. As you perused the information you should have found and highlighted problem statements that are discharge barriers. Once, you complete this task you can choose exact problem statements.

This 64-year-old, married, currently unemployed, Caucasian male was admitted to City Hospital for treatment of depression. **Mr. Landry presented to the emergency room after an overdose of Prozac in a *suicide attempt*. Mr. Landry stated, "I've got nothing to live for and I just want to die."**

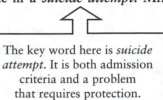

The key word here is *suicide attempt*. It is both admission criteria and a problem that requires protection.

After having his stomach pumped, Mr. Landry was stabilized medically, and referred for admission to the psychiatric service. The patient's admission status was voluntary.

This information was collected from the patient and his wife and verified with Joyce, his daughter. The information is considered reliable.

ADMISSION CRITERIA

1. The patient is a danger to himself.
2. The patient attempted suicide within the last 8 hours.
3. The patient is unable to attend to activities of daily living.

Chief Complaint

Mr. Landry feels that he has become *useless* because of his forced retirement. He feels that he has nothing to live for, and **wants to die.**

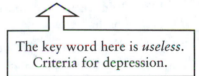

The key word here is *useless*. Criteria for depression.

Presenting Problems

The patient presents with a current history of suicidal behavior and depressive mood disturbance. Three months ago, the patient was forced to accept an early mandatory retirement from his job with Regal Paper Company. **Since that time Mr. Landry has become increasingly *withdrawn* and sullen. He spends days in his room with the blinds drawn and lying in bed. He sleeps continuously and has trouble getting out of bed. States, *"I just don't have the energy to do anything."***

The key word here is *withdrawn*. It can be stated as social isolation and withdrawal.

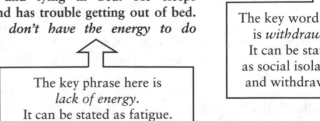

The key phrase here is *lack of energy*. It can be stated as fatigue.

At the present time, Mr. Landry is medically stable and has no physical complaints.

Affect

The patient's *affect seems somewhat blunted and flat* and he seems particularly withdrawn, tired and sad. His vocabulary seems stunted and he seems to be moving in slow motion. Mr. Landry is displaying a very narrow range of affect.

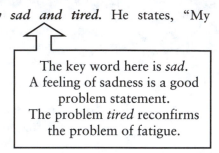

The key words here are *blunted* and *flat affect*. These are good stand-alone problem statements.

Mood

Mr. Landry describes himself as *very sad and tired*. He states, "My depression has been much worse for the last 24 hours." The patient seems disinterested in positive news.

The key word here is *sad*. A feeling of sadness is a good problem statement. The problem *tired* reconfirms the problem of fatigue.

List the Problems

Here is a list of the problems that were identified in the clinical history.

1. Suicidal attempt
2. Feeling of uselessness
3. Social isolation and withdrawal
4. Fatigue
5. Blunted and flat affect
6. Feelings of sadness

Prioritize the importance of the problems to be treated. Only treat discharge blockages.

Now, take the problems identified in the clinical history and rearrange them based on the focus of treatment and the intensity of the problem.

1. Suicide attempt
2. Social isolation and withdrawal
3. Feelings of uselessness/worthlessness
4. Blunted and flat affect
5. Fatigue

All five of these problem statements are issues that must be resolved during treatment. The treatment team would use many different therapeutic techniques, ranging from medications to talk therapies, which will help the patient deal with his or her issues. Although all five problems would be covered in an actual treatment plan, this workbook will only complete an example for the problem "Suicide Attempt," as seen in Figures 14.9 to 14.16.

Writing Additional Plans

The principles of writing a treatment plan are the same for all levels throughout the continuum of care. Documentation standards remain consistent through many different associations that govern many types of therapists.

For instance, we have discussed CMS standards repeatedly. In terms of clinical records, the major rule is that every patient must have an

Figure 14.9 | Master Treatment Plan Cover Sheet

Addressograph Imprint	**Master Treatment Plan Cover Sheet**

Case Manager	Nurse	Age	Marital Status
Larry Walker, MSW	Stephanie Johnson, RN, MN	64	Married

Legal Status	Date Master Plan Opened	Estimated LOS	Ethnic Background
Formal Voluntary	October 6, 2000	5 to 7 days	Caucasian

CRITERIA FOR ADMISSION

- ☐ Suicidal Ideation
- ☐ Suicide Plan with an Instrument
- ☑ Suicide Attempt or Gesture
- ☑ Danger to Self
- ☐ Danger to Others
- ☑ Unable to Carry out Activities of Daily Living
- ☐ Actively Psychotic
- ☐ Medical Detoxification
- ☑ Failure of Outpatient Treatment
- ☐ Active Sexual or Physical Abuse (C&A)
- ☐ Comprehensive Medical or Psychiatric Evaluation
- ☐ Medication Adjustment that must be done in a Hospital

SAFETY / RISK ANALYSIS ISSUES ON ADMISSION

Precautions for these Problem Behaviors
The patient is actively suicidal

The Patient is on the following Unit Restrictions
Mr. Landry has been placed on suicidal precautions and close observation Q15

The Patient is on the following Medical Protocols
None

INITIAL DISCHARGE PLAN

Post Discharge Living Arrangements	Physician Follow-up	Active Legal Issues Affecting Treatment
Return to Home	Dr. Gad	None

Physical Handicaps or Limitations	Dietary Problems / Special Diet	Language Barriers
None	None	None

Can the Patient Read? ☑ YES ☐ NO   Can the Patient Write? ☑ YES ☐ NO

Notes: _____

Figure 14.10 | Assessment of Strengths and Weaknesses

Assessment of Strengths and Weaknesses

Addressograph Imprint

5 4 3 2 1

☐ ☑ ☐ ☐ ☐ **Capable of independent Living**
Mr. Landry is fully capable of independent living once his suicidal attempt is resolved.

☐ ☐ ☐ ☑ ☐ **Insight / Judgment**
The patient exhibits very poor judgment at the current time. This is directly related to his depression.

☐ ☐ ☐ ☐ ☐ **Good Physical Abilities / Health**
The patient is in very good physical shape and exhibits no physical illness.

☐ ☐ ☐ ☑ ☐ **Ability to Stand up for Rights**
At the current time Mr. Landry is not able to stand up for himself. However, he has the capacity.

☐ ☑ ☐ ☐ ☐ **Community Support Network**
The patient is an active member of his church community.

☐ ☐ ☐ ☐ ☑ **Employment**
Currently, the patient is retired. He took an early, forced retirement.

☐ ☐ ☐ ☑ ☐ **Ability to express feelings**
At the current time Mr. Landry is exhibiting a blunted flat affect. He is withdrawn and has difficulty expressing his anger about the forced retirement.

☐ ☑ ☐ ☐ ☐ **Motivated for Treatment**
The patient understands the relationship between his anger and knows and wants to express his feelings in a more positive manner.

☐ ☑ ☐ ☐ ☐ **Positive Marriage**
Mr. Landry has been married for fifty years and has a very stable marriage. Part of the problem is the patient feels he has "lost face" in the marriage.

☑ ☐ ☐ ☐ ☐ **Intelligence**
The patient has above average intelligence and would be a good candidate for cognitive types of therapy.

☑ ☐ ☐ ☐ ☐ **Vocational / Occupational Skills**
Mr. Landry has many years of business and technical experience which could be put to use on a volunteer basis.

☑ ☐ ☐ ☐ ☐ **Education**
The patient is a college graduate and this would seem to be a positive indicator for the use of cognitive therapies and planning volunteer activities post-discharge.

☐ ☐ ☐ ☐ ☑ **Leisure Skills and Interests**

5=EXCELLENT   4=GOOD   3=AVERAGE   2=FAIR   1= POOR

Figure 14.11 | Axis I, II & III Diagnosis Sheet

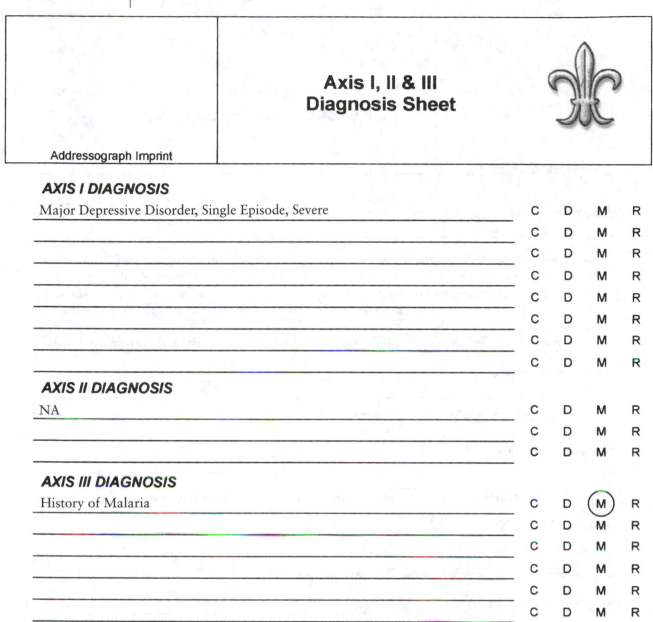

DIAGNOSIS CODES

C	This diagnosis is COMPLETED. The patient has achieved closure and the desired therapeutic results have been achieved	
D	This diagnosis is DEFERRED. Although the problem requires care, it does not need to be actively treated at this time	
M	This diagnosis is an existing problem with an existing plan of care which we will MAINTAIN	
R	This diagnosis has been identified for treatment, however the patient has REFUSED treatment	

Figure 14.12 | Axis IV Psychosocial Stressors

Axis IV Psychosocial Stressors

Addressograph Imprint

Problem with Primary Support Group: None

Death of family member, health problems in family disruption of family by separation; divorce or estrangement; removal from the home; remarriage of a parent; sexual or physical abuse parental over-protection neglect of a child;- inadequate discipline, discord with siblings; birth of a sibling.

Problem Relating to the Social Environment: Three months ago Mr. Landry was forced to take an early retirement from Regal Paper. He has felt useless and feels that he has lost stature in the family setting.

Death or loss of a friend, inadequate social support, living alone; difficulty with acculturation discrimination; adjustment to lifestyle transition (such a retirement

Educational Problems: None

Illiteracy; academic problems-, discord with teachers or classmate inadequate school or environment

Occupational Problems: None

Unemployment threat of job loss; difficult work schedule, difficult work conditions; job change discord with boss or co-workers.

Housing Problems: None

hopelessness; inadequate housing; unsafe neighborhood; discord with neighbors or landlord

Economic Problems: None

Extreme poverty inadequate finances insufficient welfare support

Problems with Access to Health Care Services: None

inadequate health care services; transportation to health care facilities unavailable, inadequate health care insurance

Problems Related to Interaction with the Legal System/Crime: None

arrest; incarceration; litigation; victim of crime

Other Psychological and Environmental Problems: None

Exposure to disease, war, other hostilities; discord with non-family care giver such as counselors, social workers or physicians, unavailability of social agencies

Figure 14.13 | Axis V GAF Scale

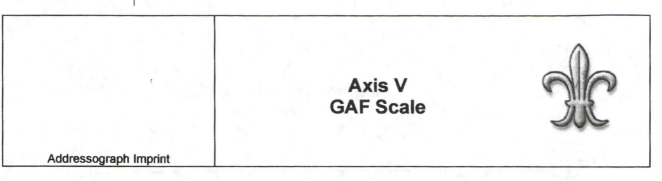

Addressograph Imprint	Axis V GAF Scale

100-91

– Superior functioning in a wide range of activities, life's problems never seem to get out of hand, is sought out by others because of his or her many positive qualities. No symptoms-

90-81

– Absent or minimal symptoms (e.g., mild anxiety before an exam), good functioning in all areas, interested and involved in a wide range of activities, socially effective, generally satisfied with life, no more than everyday problems or concerns (e.g.., an occasional argument with family members).

80-71

– If symptoms are present, they are transient and expectable reactions to psychosocial stressors (e.g., difficulty concentrating after family y argument) no more than slight impairment in social, occupational, Or school functioning (e.g., temporarily falling behind in schoolwork).

70-61

– Some Mild symptoms (e.g., depressed mood and mild insomnia) OR some difficulty in social, occupational, or school functioning (e.g., occasional truancy, or theft within the household), but generally functioning pretty well, has some meaningful interpersonal relationships

60-51

– Moderate symptoms (e.g., flat effect and circumstantial speech, occasional panic attacks, OR moderate difficulty in social, occupational, or school functioning (e.g., few friends, unable to keep a job).

50-41

– Serious symptoms (e.g., suicidal ideation, severe obsessional rituals, frequent shoplifting) OR any serious impairment in social, occupational, or school functioning, (e.g., no friends, unable to keep a job).

40-31

– Some impairment in reality testing or communication (e.g., speech is at times illogical, obscure, or irrelevant), OR major impairment in several areas, such as work or school, family relations, judgment, thinking or mood (e-g-, depressed man avoids friends, neglects family, and is unable to work, child frequently beats up younger children, is defiant at home, and is failing at school).

30-21

– Behavior is considerably influenced by delusions or hallucinations OR serious impairment In communication or judgment (e.g., sometimes incoherent, acts grossly inappropriately, suicidal preoccupation) OR inability to function in almost all areas (e.g., stays in bed all day, no job, home, friends).

20-11

– Some danger of hurting self or others (e.g., suicide attempts without dear expectation of death, frequently violent; manic excitement OR occasionally fails; to maintain minimal personal hygiene (e.g., smears feces) OR gross impairment in communication (e.g., largely incoherent or mute).

10-1

– Persistent danger of severely hurting self Or Others (recurrent violence) OR persistent inability to maintain minimal Personal hygiene OR serious suicidal act with clears expectation of death.

0

– Inadequate information

GAF Score Prior Year	GAF Score on Admission	GAF Score on Discharge
67	10	

Source: Reprinted with permission from the *Diagnostic and Statistical Manual of Mental Disorders*, Fourth Edition, Text Revision. Copyright © 2000 American Psychiatric Association.

Figure 14.14 | Master Treatment Plan Problem List

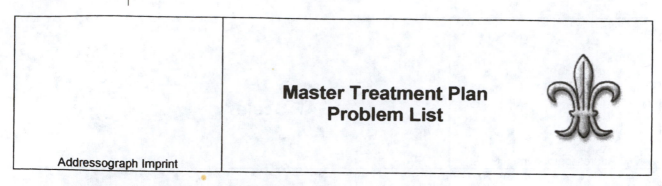

		Master Treatment Plan Problem List
Addressograph Imprint		

AXIS I&II (Psychiatric, Psychological and Problems with Mental Retardation

Date Opened	Problem #	Problem Description	Problem Status				Date Changed
08 / 06 / 00	1	Suicide Attempt	C	D	M	R	__ / __ / __
__ / __ / __	___	_____	C	D	M	R	__ / __ / __
__ / __ / __	___	_____	C	D	M	R	__ / __ / __
__ / __ / __	___	_____	C	D	M	R	__ / __ / __
__ / __ / __	___	_____	C	D	M	R	__ / __ / __
__ / __ / __	___	_____	C	D	M	R	__ / __ / __
__ / __ / __	___	_____	C	D	M	R	__ / __ / __
__ / __ / __	___	_____	C	D	M	R	__ / __ / __

AXIS III (Medical Problems)*

*Remember all Axis III diagnosis must be opened as problem statements

			Problem Status				Date Changed
__ / __ / __	___	_____	C	D	M	R	__ / __ / __
__ / __ / __	___	_____	C	D	M	R	__ / __ / __
__ / __ / __	___	_____	C	D	M	R	__ / __ / __
__ / __ / __	___	_____	C	D	M	R	__ / __ / __
__ / __ / __	___	_____	C	D	M	R	__ / __ / __
__ / __ / __	___	_____	C	D	M	R	__ / __ / __
__ / __ / __	___	_____	C	D	M	R	__ / __ / __
__ / __ / __	___	_____	C	D	M	R	__ / __ / __
__ / __ / __	___	_____	C	D	M	R	__ / __ / __

PROBLEM CODES

C	This problem is COMPLETED. The patient has achieved closure and the desired therapeutic results have been achieved	
D	This problem is DEFERRED. although the problem requires care, it does not need to be actively treated at this time	
M	This problem is an existing problem with an existing plan of care which we will MAINTAIN	
R	This problem has been identified for treatment, however the patient has REFUSED treatment	

Figure 14.15 | Problem Resolution Plan

Problem Resolution Plan

Addressograph Imprint

PROBLEM #	PROBLEM STATEMENT	DATE OPENED
1	Suicide Attempt	10/06/00

MANIFESTATIONS OF THE PROBLEM
What behaviors describes the problem?

Mr. Landry was admitted to the psychiatric service from the emergency room where his stomach had been pumped after ingesting 60–20mg Prozac in a suicide attempt. Mr. Landry stated, "I've got nothing to live for and I just want to die."

LONG TERM GOAL
How can the patient demonstrate that they can be safely discharged?

LTG #		TARGET DATE
	Mr. Landry will verbalize the absence of suicidal ideation for 48 hours prior to discharge.	

SHORT TERM GOAL
What intermediate step will be used to measure progress toward discharge goal?

STG #		TARGET DATE
	Mr. Landry will sign a written behavioral contract to notify a staff member if he has any suicidal ideation or feelings of self harm.	

#	INTERVENTIONS
	Larry Walker, MSW, will contract with Mr. Landry to notify team members if suicidal thoughts emerge. This is to be done by 10/8/00 at 2 P.M.
	Stephanie Johnson, RN, will notify all nursing personnel that Mr. Landry is on close observations Q15 minutes for suicidal precautions. She will instruct charge nurses to insure that staff watches the patient for signs of agitation, increased motor activity, unreasonable demands or request or increased anxiety and to provide measures to reassure the patient and provide a safe environment. This is to be done in daily unit activity PRN (as necessary).
	Stephanie Johnson, RN, will monitor administration of Prozac 20mg, B.I.D., via the MAR (medication administration records) as ordered by the physician. Dr. Gad will monitor the target symptomology for the clinical effectiveness of medication. This is TBD (to be done) daily.
	Christina Bonnette, MA, LPC, will help Mr. Landry explore the feelings that precipitated the suicidal attempt to help him develop better coping strategies to deal with his feelings. This is TBD in group therapy 3 times per week.

List who is responsible for this intervention by name and discipline	List the modality, milieu or treatment group used to do the intervention	Describe the focus of the intervention and the expected result of participation	List the frequency of the intervention

Figure 14.16 | Treatment Team / Patient Signature Sheet

**Treatment Team / Patient
Signature Sheet**

Addressograph Imprint

☐ Initial Planning Session ☑ Initial Treatment Team ☐ Planning Update ☐ Administrative

The Following Team Members Participated in the Interdisciplinary Treatment Plans, Reviews or Updates

Attending Physician: *Daniel W. Johnson, M.D.*

Case Manager: _____

Social Worker: *Larry Walker, M.S.W.*

Psychologist: _____

Activity Therapy: _____

Nursing: *Stephanie Johnson, R. N.*

_____

Other Allied Professional: _____

_____

_____

_____

ATTENTION
PATIENT / FAMILY INVOLVEMENT
This plan has been explained to the patient or appropriate other person.
The patient or other appropriate person has been give the opportunity to ask questions and participate in the plan for their care as documented below.

My signature attests to my participation in treatment planning and correctly documents my level of participation

☑ Contributed to Goals and Plan ☐ Present at Team Meeting ☐ Unable to Participate

☐ Aware of Plan and Contract ☐ Refused to Participate ☐ Refused to Sign Plan

Patient Signature _____*William Landry*_____ Date__10_/__6_/__00_

Family Member's Signature _____ Date____/____/____

individualized treatment plan. That belief runs through many sets of professional standards.

The Code of Ethics for the American Counseling Association states that:

Counselors and their clients work jointly in devising integrated, individualized counseling plans that offer reasonable promise of success and are consistent with the client.

Counselors and clients regularly review counseling plans to ensure their continued viability and effectiveness, respecting the client's freedom of choice.

Section B4 of the Code of Ethics for the American Counseling Association states that:

Counselors maintain records necessary for rendering professional services to their clients and as required by laws, regulations, or agency or institutional procedures. (All three taken from Herlihy, B., & Corly, G. (1997) Code of Ethics for the American Counseling Association. In ACA Ethical Standards Casebook, 5th ed. Alexandria, VA: American Counseling Association.)

As you can see, although the standards come from various sources, the substance remains the same. No matter where the patient is on the continuum of care, no matter what the therapeutic setting, no matter what type of therapist, treatment planning is necessary to provide quality care. It's good for both the patient and the therapist. These standards did not end up looking alike by happenstance. Mental health professionals have worked for years to develop a system of treatment that provides the best chance of therapeutic efficacy.

Now that we have worked with inpatient treatment planning, let us work with some outpatient plans.

There is an old story about a new social worker making his first field visit. He showed up at an elderly lady's house and was appalled by the state of dilapidation of the house. After he went inside, he discovered the woman's son was in jail for drug abuse, the husband hadn't been seen in years, the electricity had been turned off causing all the food in the refrigerator to spoil. To top it off, the woman had broken dentures.

The young social worker slumped down in his chair and said, "Mam, how in the world could I ever even begin to help you solve your problems?" She responded, "You know if I could just get my dentures fixed, I might be able to eat a little bite and then maybe I could help think my way out of this mess." The social workers eyes widened and he said, "I can get your dentures fixed." So the recovery process began.

As with all treatment planning, from outpatient to agency work the process of problem resolution is the same.

Let us review a treatment plan on the mental health center service component of the continuum of care.

MOCK CLINICAL HISTORY #2

Name: Gary Staten
DOB: 8/14/1967
Religion: Baptist

Presenting Problems

This 35-year-old, divorced, unemployed, African American male was referred from City Hospital after treatment for Polysubstance Dependence. He has had multiple admissions for drug and alcohol dependence and has had multiple failures at aftercare and applying a program of recovery.

This information was collected from the patient. The information is considered reliable.

Chief Complaint

Mr. Staten feels that he will have continued difficulty with recovery living where he does. He recognizes that the neighborhood is drug infested and that he and all of his friends live drug-oriented lifestyles.

Presenting Problems

The patient presents with a current history of alcohol and drug dependence. He is having a great deal of trouble maintaining his sobriety in his current environment. The low-income housing complex where he lives is drug infested and all of his friends use. He is unemployed, needs skills training, and suffers from symptoms of depression.

Review of Systems

The patient does not currently exhibit physical complaints and is taking multivitamins. The patient has not verbalized any physical complaints and the H&P is negative for any serious medical or surgical problems.

Past Medical History

The patient states that he has had a history of diabetes that is currently controlled by medication. Mr. Staten has been admitted to multiple hospitals and treatment clinics for alcohol and drug abuse. His drugs of choice are cocaine and alcohol.

Family History

Mr. Staten is the second of six siblings. He has one older sister and four younger brothers. All of his siblings are living but both parents are deceased. The patient's father had a long history of alcohol addiction.

Social Interaction

The patient is unmarried. He has two children, a 4-year-old son and an 8-year-old daughter. Mr. Staten dropped out of high school. Mr. Staten's sexual preference is heterosexual. He has no current, pending legal charges.

Mental Status Examination

Appearance
This 35-year-old, African American male appears somewhat older than his stated age. He is nattily dressed but is neat and clean.

Consciousness
Mr. Staten appears alert and bright.

Orientation
The patient is fully oriented to person, time, and place.

Behavior

Mr. Staten is somewhat agitated. He seems embarrassed by his situation and slumped in his chair during our interview.

Attitude

The patient's attitude is cooperative.

Affect

The patient's affect seems somewhat blunted and he seems tired and sad. His vocabulary is normal. Mr. Staten is displaying a very narrow range of affect.

Mood

Mr. Staten describes himself as very sad and tired. He describes himself as feeling hopeless. The patient seems disinterested in positive news.

Energy

The patient has a very low energy level, and currently seems somewhat disorganized.

Speech

The patient is using a very flat, monotone voice.

Thinking Process

The patient is not delusional but does seem to be obsessing on his housing situation although not inappropriately.

Perception

The patient is not experiencing any auditory, visual, or tactile hallucinations.

Medically Unexplained Somatic Symptoms

There are none and the patient denies ever assuming another personality.

Paroxysmal Attacks

Patient denies any symptoms.

Memory

The patient's short term and remote memory seems intact.

Attention and Concentration

The patient seems easily distracted and has trouble with serial 3s, a test that measures the patient's ability to repeat series of numbers or mathematical equations. It is found in the information for the psychiatric evaluation.

Intelligence and Knowledge

The patient is of above-normal intelligence. He understands abstract concepts and seems to be functioning at an average level.

Insight

The patient has insight into his problems, in that he is able to relate his alcohol and drug abuse to his current situation.

Judgment

At the current time the patient is exhibiting good judgment and is not considered a danger to himself or others.

Additional Information

Mr. Staten will be scheduled for an initial course of 20 outpatient visits.

Discharge Criteria

1. Improvement in depressive symptomology.
2. Able to verbalize a realistic plan for the future.
3. Able to verbalize new ways to manage significant relapse factors.

Preliminary Treatment Plan

1. Refer to the mental health center psychiatrist for medication evaluation and management.
2. Refer to the mental health social work department for application for Section 8 housing.
3. Continue in aftercare program at the mental health center.

Diagnostic Impressions

Axis I: Major depressive disorder, recurrent polysubstance dependence

Axis II: None

Axis III: Diabetes (controlled)

Axis IV: **Problems relating to support group**

Mr. Staten is unmarried and has no significant support.

Problems relating to social environment

Mr. Staten is enmeshed in a drug-oriented lifestyle.

Occupational problems

Mr. Staten currently is unemployed and has no significant employable skills. He is pretty much relegated to doing physical labor.

Housing problems

Mr. Staten has been living in a drug-infested housing project

Axis V: Current 45, past year 60

Recommendations for Treatment
1. Decrease depressive symptomology
2. Improve housing situation
   Begin a program of aftercare

Initial Post Discharge Information
1. Refer to AA and NA for follow-up

The patient has no physical disabilities or language restrictions and is able to read and write.

Summary

As you can see the intensity and focus of the staff interventions has changed significantly. The issues of protection have been stretched well into the patient's environment and the danger is potentially serious but not imminent.

Since we have already worked on inpatient issues (such as depression), let us use this exercise to focus our attention on environmental problems. Use the following two worksheets (Figures 14.17 and 14.18) to create problem resolution plans for Mr. Staten's environmental problems.

Create problem resolution plans for the following problems:

- Inadequate housing
- Drug-oriented lifestyle

As you can see the *process* for treatment planning remains essentially the same throughout the continuum of care (see Figures 14.19 and 14.20 for completed examples). Chapter 15 explores the use of initial treatment plans—another special circumstance for treatment planning.

Figure 14.17 | Problem Resolution Plan

	Problem Resolution Plan
Addressograph Imprint	

PROBLEM #	PROBLEM STATEMENT	DATE OPENED

MANIFESTATIONS OF THE PROBLEM
What behaviors describes the problem?

_____

_____

_____

_____

LONG TERM GOAL
How can the patient demonstrate that they can be safely discharged?

LTG #		TARGET DATE

SHORT TERM GOAL
What intermediate step will be used to measure progress toward discharge goal?

STG #		TARGET DATE

#	INTERVENTIONS

List who is responsible for this intervention by name and discipline	List the modality, milieu or treatment group used to do the intervention	Describe the focus of the intervention and the expected result of participation	List the frequency of the intervention

Figure 14.18 | Problem Resolution Plan

Problem Resolution Plan

Addressograph Imprint

PROBLEM #	PROBLEM STATEMENT	DATE OPENED

MANIFESTATIONS OF THE PROBLEM
What behaviors describes the problem?

_____

_____

_____

_____

LONG TERM GOAL
How can the patient demonstrate that they can be safely discharged?

LTG #		TARGET DATE

SHORT TERM GOAL
What intermediate step will be used to measure progress toward discharge goal?

STG #		TARGET DATE

#	INTERVENTIONS

List who is responsible for this intervention by name and discipline	List the modality, milieu or treatment group used to do the intervention	Describe the focus of the intervention and the expected result of participation	List the frequency of the intervention

Figure 14.19 | Problem Resolution Plan

	Problem Resolution Plan	
Addressograph Imprint		

PROBLEM #	PROBLEM STATEMENT	DATE OPENED
1	Living Arrangements are unacceptable because of the proximity of drug activity	9/9/01

MANIFESTATIONS OF THE PROBLEM
What behaviors describes the problem?

Mr. Staten lives is the mid-city housing project. The housing project is notorious for the level of drug sales and rampant abuse that is prevalent within the project. Mr. Staten feels that he will be unable to resist the overwhelming lure of drugs and that his program of recovery will ultimately be undermined by his home environment.

LONG TERM GOAL
How can the patient demonstrate that they can be safely discharged?

LTG #		TARGET DATE
1	Mr. Staten will understand city, state, and federal resources that he can use to impact his current living situation.	10/30/01

SHORT TERM GOAL
What intermediate step will be used to measure progress toward discharge goal?

STG #		TARGET DATE
1	Mr. Staten will commit to maintain a program of recovery regardless of his living situation.	

#	INTERVENTIONS
1	Mary Jones, MSW, will assist Mr. Staten with making a list of possible resources to explore for housing options. This is to be done in a 1:1 session by 9/30/01.
2	Ben Southworth, LVC (licensed vocational counselor), will assist patient to write a plan for seeking new housing and to apply for session 8 (low income) housing assistance. This is to be done in a 1:1 session by 9/30/01.
3	Mary Jones, MSW, will help Mr. Staten follow a commitment to sobriety during the period of time he is working on alternative living arrangements. This is to be done in aftercare 2 times per week.

List who is responsible for this intervention by name and discipline	List the modality, milieu or treatment group used to do the intervention	Describe the focus of the intervention and the expected result of participation	List the frequency of the intervention

Figure 14.20 | Problem Resolution Plan

	Problem Resolution Plan	
Addressograph Imprint		

PROBLEM #	PROBLEM STATEMENT	DATE OPENED
1	Mr. Staten only associates with people enmeshed in a Drug-Oriented Lifestyle	

MANIFESTATIONS OF THE PROBLEM
What behaviors describes the problem?

Mr. Staten has trouble with the recovery process because his associates are fully engaged in a drug-oriented lifestyle. He is concerned about the relationship between his interaction with his peers and possible "triggers" to relapse.

LONG TERM GOAL
How can the patient demonstrate that they can be safely discharged?

LTG #		TARGET DATE
1	Mr. Staten will begin to learn the essential social skills necessary to form new relationships with non-users.	12/30/00

SHORT TERM GOAL
What intermediate step will be used to measure progress toward discharge goal?

STG #		TARGET DATE
1	Mr. Staten will express an understanding of how his previous relationships have been maladaptive.	11/30/00

#	INTERVENTIONS
1	Larry Walker, MSW, will have Mr. Staten identify situations the patient manipulated in order to abuse substances and how they were related to his environment. This is to be done by 10/8/00 at 2 P.M.
2	Christina Bonnette, MA, LPC, will help Mr. Staten identify friends/companions and the reasons for his friendships with these people. This is TBD in a 1:1 session by 10/15/00.
3	Larry Walker, MSW, will point out to Mr. Staten when his interactions are manipulative or maladaptive so that he can begin to understand the relationship between these behaviors and making poor choices for friends/associates. This is to be done in aftercare 2 times per week.

List who is responsible for this intervention by name and discipline	List the modality, milieu or treatment group used to do the intervention	Describe the focus of the intervention and the expected result of participation	List the frequency of the intervention

The better part of valour is discretion . . .
— **William Shakespeare**

The proof of the pudding is in the testing.
— **Miguel de Cervantes**

Initial Treatment Plans | 15

WHAT IS AN INITIAL TREATMENT PLAN?

You can look in the current CMS guidelines and never see a requirement for an initial treatment plan. In times past, when lengths of stays were longer, HCFA (the forerunner of CMS) required an initial treatment plan within 3 days and a master treatment plan within 10 days. In the current reimbursement environment where therapeutic time is a precious commodity, treatment teams cannot wait 10 days to do a treatment plan; if they did, most of their patients would be discharged before the plan was ever written.

When managed care necessitated shorter lengths of stay, CMS changed the length of time a treatment team had to complete a *master* treatment plan from 10 days to 72 hours. Because CMS initially dictated that an initial plan for care be completed in 72 hours, this requirement was dropped. Most surveyors feel that opening a master treatment plan in 72 hours is adequate. However, in the real world, there is always an exception to the plan. On occasion, surveyors request an initial treatment plan to be completed within 24 hours, *even though there is no specific standard that requires this task.*

To survive a survey, the treatment team has to be flexible and always remember Surveyor's Rule Number Two:

Do not argue with a surveyor; it is not productive and you *cannot* win.

Surveyors are usually more knowledgeable about treatment planning than the staff of the facility being surveyed. When surveyors do not like what they see in the documentation, they start looking deeper in the chart and digging into a larger variety of issues. When they start requesting special documentation, there is usually a "method to the madness."

Surveyors request "additional documentation" when they cannot find adequate documentation verifying that standards are being met or that individual therapeutic issues are being properly managed.

If a surveyor asks for additional documentation that seems out of the ordinary, do not argue; the best course of action is to first respond positively to the request and argue later. Arguing with a surveyor is not productive.

Unless the request is unethical or illegal, or endangers the patient, arguing with the surveyor is just not a smart strategy.

Specifically, the reason surveyors request an initial plan of care is to justify active treatment. Remember CMS standards state:

> **"Active treatment is an essential requirement for inpatient psychiatric care. Active treatment is a clinical process involving the ongoing assessment, diagnosis, intervention, evaluation of care, and treatment and planning under the direction of a psychiatrist."** ↩ B125

If surveyors do not feel that active care is being documented, they may ask for an initial care plan to further a point. They expect the staff to document the presence of active treatment and to be able to show a plan that ensures the patient's safety. Additionally, surveyors want documentation that the treatment team has a plan to manage the patient's problems and behavior until the master plan is complete. In other words:

1. They want to make sure that the first 3 days of treatment are not wasted.
2. They want to ensure that the patient is receiving active treatment for the payment received.
3. Finally, and most importantly, they want to see that the staff protects the patient.

INITIAL CARE PLANS

Initial care plans are simply abbreviated versions of the master treatment plan. They are written to ensure that the patient is protected as necessary until the entire team can evaluate the situation and write the master treatment plan. Generally, the first sheet of an initial care plan will deal with transmitting information about the patient's safety and status.

- Is the patient on suicidal precautions?
- Do they have a language restriction?
- Can the patient read or write?
- Has the patient been placed on any unit restrictions?
- Are there any serious medical problems?
- Is the patient an elopement risk?
- Are there pending legal issues?
- Does the patient have any transmittable disease?

Each of these problems needs immediate staff intervention and management. The Initial Treatment Plan Cover Sheet (Figure 15.1) provides the treatment team with a quick overview of the patient. Additionally, it provides a checklist to make sure certain items are addressed in a timely manner.

Figure 15.2 is an example of the face sheet used for an initial plan of care. The face sheet also provides a central focal point of information for the nursing staff and therapist.

After the initial face sheet is completed, the staff should begin to concentrate on the problems that require the staff to protect or stabilize the patient. Remember, the definition of a hospital is a facility that provides nursing, medical, and therapeutic interventions 24 hours a day, 7 days a week. This also defines the requirements for admission; therefore, it stands to reason that the protection issues come first.

Figure 15.1 | Initial Treatment Plan Cover Sheet

Initial Treatment Plan Cover Sheet

Addressograph Imprint

Attending Physician	Nurse Manager	Admission Diagnosis

Legal Status	Date Initial Plan Opened	Estimated LOS	Nursing Signature

Medical / Nursing Precautions

☐ Suicidal Precautions
☐ Seizure Precautions
☐ Isolation
☐ HIV +
Hepatitis ☐ A ☐ B ☐ C
☐ PPD
☐ Allergies _____

Withdrawal Protocols

☐ Alcohol
☐ Benzodiazipines
☐ Opioid
☐ Other

_____

Special Dietary Orders

_____

Other Medical Issues

_____

Risk Analysis Issues

☐ Potential for Falling
☐ Potential for Elopement
☐ Potential for Sexual Acting Out
☐ Potential for Infection Related to:

_____

☐ Unable to carry out ADL's
☐ Potential Danger to Self
☐ Potential danger to Others
☐ Confused Behavior
☐ Actively Psychotic
  Hallucinations
  ☐ Command
  ☐ Auditory
  ☐ Tactile
  ☐ Visual

Special Needs / Accommodations

Visual Impairments
☐ Blind
☐ Wears Glasses

Hearing Impairments
☐ Hard of Hearing (HOH)
☐ Deaf

Language or Speech Impairments
☐ Mute
☐ Speaks a foreign Language _____
☐ Needs a Translator
☐ Needs someone to sign

Language or Speech Impairments
☐ Mute
☐ Speaks a foreign Language _____
☐ Needs a Translator

Equipment Needs
☐ Walker
☐ Wheelchair
☐ Prosthetic Devices
☐ Other _____

Legal Issues

☐ Court Date Scheduled _____ / _____ / _____
☐ Probation Meeting _____ / _____ / _____
☐ Legal Hold For Discharge
☐ Court Ordered Treatment for: _____

Restrictions and Limitations

☐ Limit Visitation
☐ Limit Phone use
☐ Restricted to Unit
☐ Notes:_____

_____

Figure 15.2 | An Example of the Face Sheet for an Initial Treatment Plan

Patient Name	Nurse Manager	Admission Diagnosis

The Initial Goal for This Problem is to: ☐ **Protect** ☐ **Stabilize**   Date:_____ / _____ / _____

Problem Statement: _____

Interventions

_____

_____

_____

_____

_____

_____

_____

_____

_____

_____

Nursing Signature: _____

Let's review the partial list of problems from the patient's acuity scale that require staff protection.

EXAMPLES OF POSSIBLE PROBLEMS OR BEHAVIORS

- Aggressive behavior
- Anorexia
- Compulsive ritualistic behavior
- Confusion
- Paranoid delusions
- Drug/food interaction
- Disorientation
- Erratic emotional displays
- Fire setting
- Flight of ideas
- Auditory, tactile, and visual hallucinations
- High risk for trauma
- Inability to communicate
- Serious medical problems
- Obsessive thoughts
- Panic attacks
- Potential for falling
- Suicide attempt
- Self-mutilating behavior
- Psychomotor agitation
- Recurrent thoughts of death
- Self-care deficit
- Self-destructive behavior
- Seizures
- Sexual abuse (active)
- Persistent suicidal ideation

As you can see, each of these problems requires immediate intervention to prevent the patient from imminent harm. Since this is the highest intensity of staff intervention, the universal acuity scale will start here at its high point. Because these problems require immediate intervention they are the type of problems the treatment team should address on the initial treatment plan.

Because the time frame to complete initial treatment plans is short, the interventions described in these plans are usually completed by the nursing staff. Since the plan's immediate purpose is to protect or stabilize the patient, the long-term and short-term goals for an initial plan of care will be reduced to a statement that the goal of the interventions is to either protect or stabilize the patient. There is no a manifestation statement. Figure 15.2 depicts a second page of the initial treatment plan.

Initially, the object is for the team to address all of the problems that would present immediate danger to the patient, unit, or staff. Once the staff has decided what interventions they will use, the plan would be completed as usual.

Remember, the main object of the *initial* treatment plan is:

1. To provide a safe environment for the patient
2. To document the implementation of an immediate plan of care
3. To document the patient's reaction to the interventions, and active management of the patient's care until the master treatment plan is completed.

CHAPTER 15 SELF-TEST

Answer the following questions. When you have completed the test, check your answers in Appendix B.

1. What circumstances would most likely prompt a surveyor to ask for an initial treatment plan?

2. What is the purpose of an initial treatment plan?

3. What is meant by the term *active treatment*?

4. What is Surveyor Rule Number Two?

5. What is the difference between writing interventions for initial care plans and writing them for the master treatment plan?

Method will teach you to win time . . .
— **Johann Wolfgang von Goethe**

Forms

Function follows form.

WHY USE FORMS?

If the best treatment plan is a blank piece of paper, what is the purpose of forms? A previous chapter detailed CMS's position that the best treatment planning form is a blank piece of paper. What CMS surveyors mean by this statement is that they want the treatment team or therapist to write flexible and individualized care plans. They do *not* want "canned plans" or plans that all give patients the same therapy despite the uniqueness of their specific problems. If everyone were the same, we could just photocopy treatment plans (and incidentally some treatment facilities do), but people are different and so their care plans should be individualized to meet their specific needs.

To assure the treatment team includes all the required information that needs to be included in the treatment plan, here are some suggested forms that will help team members meet CMS guidelines. These forms are intended to be used as guides. CMS clearly states that there is no single acceptable format for a treatment plan.

The included forms and their purposes are:

Master Treatment Plan Cover Sheet   This form is intended to outline and summarize basic patient information in a single, easy-to-find format. It will advise the reader regarding who is involved in the plan, any precautions to be taken, and preliminary discharge planning.

Assessment of Strengths and Weaknesses   This form helps the therapist identify blockages to treatment, as well as define individual patient strengths that can be built upon to craft successful treatment. The form is both qualitative and quantitative in design. Remember that CMS considers a "patient strength" to be an attribute that can be utilized and built upon to begin the recovery process.

Axis I, II and III—Diagnosis Status Sheet   This form is used to outline and give details regarding the progress of all of the patient's treatment diagnoses.

It also gives a quick synopsis of the ongoing progress made toward treating each diagnosis. The use of a series of progress codes helps the staff translate the immediate status of all the diagnoses.

Axis IV—Psychosocial Stressors   This form outlines the specific areas of reference (as designated by the *DSM–IV-TR*) for inclusion in this evaluation.

Axis V—The GAF Scale   This form spells out the global assessment of functioning scale as defined in the *DSM–IV-TR*.

Master Treatment Plan Problem List   This form is used to delineate the problems the treatment team has designated for treatment and the progress made toward resolving each of these problems.

Problem Resolution Plan   This form is the focal point of the treatment plan. It is used to find answers to the following questions:
  a. What is the problem and what does it look like in my patient?
  b. What would the patient have to accomplish to satisfy the requirements to move up in the continuum of care?
  c. What specifically is the staff going to do to help the patient resolve this problem?

Problem Resolution Plan Continuation Sheet   This form is used to continue recording information when the initial treatment plan sheet is not sufficient for the purpose.

Problem Resolution Plan Update   This form is used to document the active progress or lack of progress at subsequent treatment team meetings.

Treatment Team Signature Sheet   This form is used to document for the record when the treatment team meetings were held. Basic information should include which members of the treatment team attended the meeting (by name and discipline), as well as document the patient's progress and participation in his or her plan of care.

With the exception of the material for the forms to record Axis IV and V, the following forms are the property of Behavioral Health Management Services, LLC. They are used by Brooks/Cole as illustrations in this workbook and may be used by teaching institutions during class and for assignments.

For permission to use these forms please call or write:

Behavioral Health Management Services, LLC
6441 Canal Boulevard
New Orleans, LA 70124
(504) 488-2539

For permission to use the material in the forms to record Axiv IV and V, please write:

American Psychiatric Association
1400 K Street, NW
Washington, DC 20005

To learn more about our computer-assisted treatment planning program and other clinical products, visit our Web site at www.sof-serve.com.

The nice thing about standards is that there are so many to choose from.
— Andrew S. Tanenbaum

Appendix A: CMS Standards and Attestation Statements

He who has the gold rules.

SPECIAL CONDITIONS OF PARTICIPATION

The majority of this workbook describes ways to meet the CMS standards for psychiatric hospitals. The irony of this is that most providers have never seen the CMS standards. Anyone would probably agree that a hospital would have a hard time attesting that it meets standards it has never seen.

In the real world, CMS sometimes contracts with state survey teams to manage the compliance survey process. Other times, CMS will send in a survey team employed by CMS. In either case, due to a shortage of survey staff, facilities may not see a survey team for years. This does not relieve them from the responsibility of seeing that the appropriate standards of care are met.

To cover this lapse in the survey process, CMS sends out attestation statements. Every year facilities that participate in the Medicare Psychiatric Program are sent a form called an attestation statement. The facility receives this form in lieu of an on-site survey. This form essentially asks the providers to attest (swear) that they have continued to provide patient treatment that meets with the CMS standards of care.

This attestation statement has the same force as a compliance survey. Even though there is a description of the standards, some facilities do not have an adequate grasp of the standards to know how to realistically answer the questions.

The full CMS survey standards include the tag number, which identifies the standard, and a guidance, which explains the intent of the regulation. Furthermore, there are survey probes that are intended to be a practical guidance to the surveyors. These probes point out specifics that indicate the regulation is being followed. It is imperative that facilities become familiar with these standards.

For future reference, here are the CMS clinical records standards in their entirety.

MEDICARE SPECIAL CONDITIONS OF PARTICIPATION

Clinical Records Standards

TAG NUMBER	REGULATION	GUIDANCE TO SURVEYORS
B98	§482.60 Conditions of Participation: Special provisions applying to psychiatric hospitals. Psychiatric hospitals must—	
B99	(a) Be primarily engaged in providing, by or under the supervision of a doctor of medicine or osteopathy, psychiatric services for the diagnosis and treatment of mentally ill persons.	§482.60(a) GUIDANCE: The hospital will be deemed to meet standard a) if it meets standards (c) and (d).
B100	(b) Meet the Conditions of Participation specified in §§482.1 through 482.23 and §§482.25 through 482.57;	§482.60(b) GUIDANCE: The hospital is either accredited by JCAHO or AOA; or meets the Condition of Participation for Hospitals, §§482.1 through 482.23 and and §§482.25 through 482.57.
B101	(c) Maintain clinical records on all patients, including records sufficient to permit HCFA to determine the degree and intensity of treatment furnished to Medicare beneficiaries, as specified in§482.61; and	
B102	(d) Meet the staffing requirements specified in §482.62.	
B103	§482.61 Condition of Participation: Special medical record requirements for psychiatric hospitals The medical records maintained by a psychiatric hospital must permit determination of the degree and intensity of the treatment provided to individuals who are furnished services in the institution.	§482.61 GUIDANCE: The clinical record should provide information that indicates need for admission and treatment, treatment goals, changes in status of treatment and discharge planning, and follow-up and the outcomes experienced by patients. The structure and content of the individual patient's record must be an accurate functional representation of the actual experience of the individual in the facility. It must contain enough information to indicate that the facility knows the status of the patient, has adequate plans to intervene, and provides sufficient evidence of the effects of the intervention, and how their

B103 *(continued)*		interventions served as a function of the outcomes experienced. You must be able to identify this through interviews with staff, and when possible with individuals being served, as well as through observations.
	(a) Standard: Development of assessment/diagnostic data.	
B104	Medical records must stress the psychiatric components of the record, including history of findings and treatment provided for the psychiatric condition for which the patient is hospitalized.	
B105	(1) The identification data must include the patient's legal status.	§482.61(a)(1) GUIDANCE: Definition: Legal Status is defined in the State statutes and dictates the circumstances under which the patient was admitted and/or is being treated—i.e., voluntary, involuntary, committed by court, evaluation and recertification are in accordance with state requirements. Determine through interview with hospital staff the terminology they use in defining "legal status." If evaluation and recertification is required by the State, determine that legal documentation supporting this status is present. Changes in legal status should also be recorded with the date of change.
B106	(2) A provisional or admitting diagnosis must be made on every patient at the time of admission, and must include the diagnosis of intercurrent diseases as well as the psychiatric diagnosis.	§482.61(a)(2) GUIDANCE: There is an admission or working psychiatric diagnosis (including rule-out diagnoses) written in the most current edition of the American Psychiatric Association's Diagnostic and and Statistical Manual (DSM) or the approved International Classification of Diseases (ICD) nomenclature. This diagnosis is made and entered into the chart of each patient at the time of the admission examination. The final diagnosis may differ from the initial diagnosis if subsequent evaluation and observation support a change. If a diagnosis is absent, there must be justification for its absence. For example, if a patient was psychotic on admission and was not accompanied by family or significant others. Intercurrent (other than psychiatric) diagnoses must be documented when they are made. Attention should be paid to physical examination notes, including known medical conditions, even allergies and recent exposure to infections, illness, or substance abuse, and to available

| B106 (continued) | | laboratory or test reports which identify abnormal findings to see that these are reflected by appropriate diagnosis.

These diagnoses may be found in a variety of locations in the medical record, e.g., the identification/face sheet, the finding of admission physical examination, the psychiatric evaluation the "admission work up" or the physician's progress notes. Diagnostic categories should include physical illness when present.

§82.61 (a) (2) PROBES

Are abnormal physical examination findings and/or laboratory findings justified by further diagnostic testing and/or development of an intercurrent diagnosis, and, if so, was such done?

If an identified physical illness requires immediate treatment, is the treatment being given?

How will an identified physical illness be likely to impact on the patient's eventual outcome? To what extent has this potential impact been addressed by the team? |
| --- | --- | --- |
| B107 | (3) The reasons for admission must be clearly documented as stated by the patient and/or others significantly involved. | §482.61(a)(3) GUIDANCE:

The purpose of this regulation is to provide an understanding of what caused the patient to come to the hospital, and the patient's response to admission.

The hospital records the statements and reason for admission given by family and by others, as well as the patient (preferably verbatim), with informant identified, in a variety of locations, e.g., in transfer and admission notes from the physician, nurses and social workers.

Records should not contain vague, ill-defined reports from unknown sources. Records should record "who", "what", "where", "when", and "why." |
| | | §482.61 (a) (3) PROBES:

Can the patient describe problems, stresses, situations experienced prior to hospitalization or do they still exist?

Who is the informant?

Did the informant witness the patient's behavior? If not, on what basis has the informant come to know the patient's behavior?

Has staff elicited whether the patient has exhibited similar behavior previously? If so, what was different this time to make hospitalization necessary? |

B107 (continued)		Were there other changes/events in the patient's environment (death, separations of significant others) which contributed to the need for hospitalization? If so, has staff explored how these will impact in the patient's treatment? Has this been addressed by the treatment team? Has there been an interruption or change in the patient's medication which may have been a factor in the patient's hospitalization?
B108	(4) The social service records, including reports of interviews with patients, family members, and others, must provide an assessment of home plans and family attitudes, and community resource contacts as well as a social history.	(4) GUIDANCE: The purpose of the social work assessment is to determine the current baseline social functioning (strengths and deficits) of the patient, from which treatment interventions and discharge plans are to be formulated. Patient length of stay is a key factor influencing hospital documentation policy, i.e., establishing timeframes for completion, documentation, and filing of the psychosocial assessment, and treatment planning in the medical record. A psychosocial history/assessment must be completed on all patients. Three key components to be addressed: A. Factual and Historical Information 1. Specific reasons for the patient's admission or readmission; 2. A description of the patient's past and present biopsychosocial functioning; 3. Family and marital history, dynamics, and patient's relationships with family and significant others; 4. Pertinent religious and cultural factors; 5. History of physical, sexual and emotional abuse; 6. Significant aspects of psychiatric, medical, and substance abuse history and treatment as presented by family members and significant others; 7. Educational, vocational, employment, and military service history; 8. Identification of community resources including previously used treatment sources; 9. Identification of present environmental and financial needs

B108 *(continued)*		B. Social Evaluation 1. Patient strength and deficits; 2. High risk psychosocial issues requiring early treatment planning and intervention—i.e., unattended child(ren) in home; prior noncompliance to specific treatment and/ or discharge interventions; and potential obstacles to present treatment and discharge planning.
		C. Conclusions and Recommendations Assessment of Sections A and B shall result in the development of (C) recommendations related to the following areas: 1. Anticipated necessary steps for discharge to occur; 2. High risk patient and/or family psychosocial issues requiring early treatment planning and immediate intervention regardless of the patient's length of stay; 3. Specific community resources/ support systems for utilization in discharge planning—i.e., housing, living arrangements, financial aid, and aftercare treatment sources; 4. Anticipated social work role(s) in treatment and discharge planning.
		§482.61 (a) (4) PROBES Does the psychosocial history/assessment indicate: 1. Clear identification of the informant(s) and sources of information? 2. Whether information is considered reliable? 3. Patient participation to the extent possible in provision of data relative to treatment and discharge planning? 4. Integration of significant data including identified high risk psychosocial issues (problems) into the treatment plan? How does the hospital insure the information is reliable?
B109	(5) When indicated, a complete neurological examination must be recorded at the time of the admission physical examination.	§482.61(a)(5) GUIDANCE: Upon admission the patient should receive a thorough history and physical examination with all indicated laboratory examinations. These investigations must be sufficient to discover all structural, functional, systemic and metabolic

B109
(continued)

disorders. A thorough history of the patient's past physical disorders, head trauma, accidents, substance dependence/abuse, exposure to toxic agents, tumors, infections, seizures or temporary loss of consciousness, and headaches, will alert the physician to look for the presence of continuing pathology or possible sequelae any of which may turn out to be significant and pertinent to the present mental illness. Equally important is a thorough physical examination to look for signs of any current illness since psychotic symptoms may be due to a general medical condition or substance related disorder.

The screening neurologic examination

As part of the physical examination, the physician will perform a "screening" neurologic examination. While there is no precise definition of a screening neurologic examination in medical practice such examination is expected to assess gross function of the various divisions of the central nervous system as opposite to detailed, fine testing of each division. Gross testing of Cranial Nerves II through XII should be included. Statements such as "Cranial Nerves II to XII intact" are not acceptable. These areas may be found in various parts of the physical examination and not just grouped specifically under the neurologic.

In any case where a system review indicate positive neurologic symptomatology, a more detailed examination would be necessary, with neurologic work-up or consultation ordered as appropriate after the screening neurologic examination was completed.

Complete neurologic examination.

A complete, comprehensive neurologic examination includes a review of the patient's history, physical examination and for psychiatric patients, a review of the psychiatric evaluation. The neurologist/psychiatrist himself/herself also takes a history to obtain the necessary information not already available in the medical record or referral form. The neurologic examination is a detailed, orderly survey of the various sections of the nervous system. As an example, whereas a simple reading of a printed page will be sufficient to assess grossly the patient's sight (cranial nerve II) in a complete neurologic examination, the neurologist may test visual acuity with a snellen chart, perform a fundoscopic examination of both eyes (sometimes after dilating the pupils) and he/she will examine the patient's visual fields. In the examination of the motor system, the power of muscle groups of the extremities, the neck and trunk are tested. Where an indication of diminished strength is noted, testing of smaller muscle groups and even individual muscles are

B109 *(continued)*		tested. In a complete neurologic examinations all the systems are examined, but the physician will emphasize even more the areas pertinent to the problem for which the examination was requested. §482.61(a)(5) PROBES: Did the presence of an abnormal physical finding or laboratory finding justify the need for further diagnostic testing, or for the development of an intercurrent diagnosis? If the finding justified further follow-up in either situation, was such follow-up done? Is there evidence that a screening neurologic examination was done and recorded at the time of the physical examination? Was the screening neurologic or history indicative of possible involvement (tremors, paralysis, motor weakness or muscle atrophy, severe headaches, seizures, head trauma? If indicated, was a complete, comprehensive neurologic exam ordered, completed and recorded in the medical record in a timely manner?
	(b) Standard: Psychiatric evaluation	
B110	Each patient must receive a psychiatric evaluation that must—	§482.61(b) GUIDANCE: The psychiatric evaluation is done for the purpose of determining the patient's diagnosis and treatment and, therefore, it must contain the necessary information to justify the diagnosis and planned treatment. The psychiatric evaluation is a total appraisal or assessment of the patient's illness. It is the physician's assessment of the contributing factors and forces in the evolution of the patient's illness including the patient's perception of his or her illness. Through the psychiatric evaluation the physician seeks to secure a biographical-historical perspective of the patient's personality, with a clear psychological picture of the patient as a specific human being with his or her individual problems. While performing the psychiatric evaluation, the physician reaches an understanding of the patient's basic personality structure, of the patient's developmental period, of his or her value systems, of his or her past medical history including surgical procedures and other treatments, his or her past psychological traumatic experiences, his or her defense mechanisms, his or her supporting systems, any precipitating factors and how all these may have impacted and interplayed with each other to

B110
(continued)

result in the present illness. In the psychiatric evaluation the patient should emerge as a dynamic human being with a past, a present and a potential future with a thread of logical continuity.

The psychiatric evaluation includes all the requirements described in this standard and the information necessary to justify the diagnosis and treatment. A physician's signature is necessary. In those cases where the mental status portion of the psychiatric evaluation is performed by a non-physician, there should be evidence that the person is credentialed by the hospital, legally authorized by the State to perform that function, and a physician review and countersignature is present, where required by hospital policy or State law.

In order to satisfy the requirements §482.61 (b)(1–7) of this standard, and to meet the standards of medical practice, the psychiatric evaluation should include the following component parts:

§482.61(b) PROBES:

1—The patient's chief complaints and/or reaction to hospitalization, recorded in patient's own words where possible.

Why is the patient in the hospital?

Was it his/her idea? (Does he/she feel ill/disturbed/frightened?)

Is the patient in the hospital against his/her will? Who decided to hospitalize/why?

2—Past history of any psychiatric problems and treatment, including prior precipitating factors, diagnosis, course and treatment.

Has the patient been chronically ill? Continuously/repeatedly?

How severely has the past illness/treatment interfered with the patient's development and/or adjustment?

Are there persistent symptoms/signs/behaviors which must be addressed and treated in order to favorably impact on the future psychiatric course?

What medications or supports helped him/her improve in the past? Are the same resources available to impact on the patient's treatment during this episode?

3—Past family, educational, vocational, occupational and social history.

| B110 (continued) | | To what extent, if any, is there a presence or absence of familial predisposition?

What is the patient's educational level? Was he/she a good student? Is he/she still interested in learning?

What jobs has the patient held? For how long? Is he/she now employed/unemployed? For how long? Has he/she ever worked?

How does the patient get along with people? As a child, did he/she have friends? Does he/she have friends now?

4—Within the psychiatric evaluation does one find the specific signs and symptoms, and other factors, that justify the diagnosis? |
|---|---|---|
| B111 | (1) Be completed within 60 hours of admission; | |
| B112 | (2) Include a medical history; | §482.61(b)(2) GUIDANCE:

The psychiatric evaluation must include the non-psychiatric medical history including physical disabilities, mental retardation and treatment.

§482.61(b)(2) PROBES:

Does the evaluation include:

Relevant past surgery? Past medical conditions and disabilities especially those of a chronic nature?

Have these contributed to the patient's psychiatric condition? How?

Are any of these conditions still present to any significant degree? Are they likely to impact on the patient's recovery/remission? Should they be addressed immediately? Does the facility have the capability to intervene? If not, how is the need to be met? |
| B113 | (3) Contain a record of mental status; | §482.61(b)(3) GUIDANCE:

The mental status must describe the appearance and behavior, emotional response, verbalization, thought content, and cognition of the patient as reported by the patient and observed by the examiner at the time of the examination. This description is appropriate to the patient's condition.

Explore the mental status for descriptions of the patient's presentation during the examination that are relevant to the diagnosis and treatment of the patient. An example of a portion of the patient interview: "The patient periodically states the |

B113 (continued)		examiner's name correctly during this examination after hearing it once, accurately describes his past history in great detail, precisely characterizes his present situation, can list events in logical sequence that have led to his present illness, but believes that his pre-admission insomnia, anorexia, and 35 pound weight loss over the past four months are totally the result of his sexual promiscuity of ten years ago and have nothing to do with his concurrent use of 50 to 60 mg. of Amphetamine daily." From this information one can conclude that the patient is oriented, his memory is intact, but that he has poor judgment and no insight. It is not acceptable just to write "oriented, memory intact, judgement poor, and insight nil", without any supportive information.
B114	(4) Note the onset of illness and the circumstances leading to admission;	§482.61(b)(4) GUIDANCE: In a hospitalized patient, the identified problem should be related to the patient's need for hospital admission. The psychiatric evaluation includes a history of present illness, including onset, precipitating factors and reason for the current admission, signs and symptoms, course, and the results of any treatment received. §482.61(b)(4) PROBES: How long has the patient been ill? Was it a gradual or sudden onset? Is this a recurrence? What were the precipitating factors? What happened? What symptoms, signs, behaviors made this hospitalization necessary? What treatment has the patient already received before coming to the hospital? Is any medication he received listed?
B115	(5) Describe attitudes and behavior;	§482.61(b)(5) GUIDANCE: The problem statement should describe behavior(s) which require change in order for the patient to function in a less restrictive setting. The identified problems may also include behavioral or relationship difficulties with significant others which require active treatment in order to facilitate a successful discharge.
B116	(6) Estimate intellectual functioning, memory functioning and orientation;	§482.61(b)(6) GUIDANCE: Refer to §482.61(b)(3)
	and	

B117	(7) Include an inventory of the patient's assets in descriptive, not interpretive fashion.	§482.61(b)(7) GUIDANCE: Although the term strength is often used interchangeably with assets, only the assets describe personal factors on which to base the treatment plan or which are useful in therapy represent personal strengths. Strengths are personal attributes i.e., knowledge, interests, skills, aptitudes, personal experiences, education, talents and employment status, which may be useful in developing a meaningful treatment plan. For purposes of the regulation, words such as "youth," "pretty," "Social Security income," and "has a car" do not represent assets. (See also §482.61(c)(1).)
	(c) Standard: Treatment Plan.	
B118	Each patient must have an individual comprehensive treatment plan	§482.61 (c)(1) GUIDANCE: The patient and treatment team collaboratively develop the patient's treatment plan. The treatment plan is the outline of what the hospital has committed itself to do for the patient, based on an assessment of the patient's needs. The facility selects its format for treatment plans and treatment plan updates. §482.61(c)(1) SURVEY PROCEDURE: Determination of compliance regarding treatment plans is accomplished by the surveyor using the following methods, and to the extent possible, the following order: (1) Observation of the patient and staff at planned therapies/meetings, in various settings both on and off the patient units, in formal and informal staff-patient interactions and in a variety of daily settings; (2) Interviews with patients, families, treatment staff and others involved directly or indirectly with active treatment; (3) Reviews of scheduled treatment programs (individual, group, family meetings, therapeutic activities, therapeutic procedures); (4) Attendance at multidisciplinary treatment planning meetings, if time permits; and (5) Medical record review. §482.61(c)(1) PROBE: Has the information gained from assessing/evaluating the patient been utilized to create an individualized treatment plan?

B119	The plan must be based on an inventory of the patient's strengths and disabilities.	§482.61(c)(1) GUIDANCE:

§482.61(c)(1) GUIDANCE:

A disability is any psychiatric, biopsychosocial problem requiring treatment/intervention. The term disability and problem are used inter-changeably. The treatment plan is derived from the information contained in the psychiatric evaluation and in the assessments/diagnostic data collected by the total treatment team. Based on the assessment summaries formulated by team members of various disciplines, the treatment team identifies which patient disabilities will be treated during hospitalization. Patient strengths which can be utilized in treatment must be identified. (See also §482.61(b)(7).)

Treatment planning depends on several variables; whether the admission is limited to crisis intervention, short-term treatment or long-term treatment. The briefer the hospital stay, the fewer disciplines may be involved in the patient's treatment.

There must be evidence of periodic review of the patient's response and progress toward meeting planned goals. If the patient has made progress toward meeting goals, or if there is a lack of progress, the review must justify: (1) continuing with the current goals and approaches; or (2) revising the treatment plan to increase the possibility of a successful treatment outcome.

Consideration must be given to the type of psychiatric program(s) under review to determine the timeframe for treatment plan review. The interval within which treatment plan reviews are conducted is determined by the hospital, however, the hospital's review system must be sufficiently responsive to ensure the treatment plan is reviewed: whenever a goal(s) has been accomplished; when a patient is regressing; when a patient is failing to progress; or when a patient requires a new treatment goal. The facility is expected to pursue aggressively the attendance of all relevant participants at the team meetings. Question any routine and regular absences of individuals who would be expected to attend.

§482.61(c)(1) PROBES:

Is the treatment plan individualized, i.e., patient-specific, or is there a predictable sameness from plan to plan?

When packaged plans or programs are used, do staff include needed individual adaptations in the plan?

Are the patient's observed behaviors consistent with the problems and strengths identified in the plan or update?

B119 (continued)		Have the views which the patient communicated to the surveyor regarding problems which require treatment during hospitalization and plans for discharge, been incorporated in the plan or update?
	The written plan must include—	
B120	(i) A substantiated diagnosis;	§482.61(c)(1)(i) GUIDANCE: The substantiated diagnosis serves as the basis for treatment interventions. A substantiated diagnosis is the diagnosis identified by the treatment team to be the primary focus upon which treatment planning will be based. It evolves from the synthesis of data from various disciplines. At the time of admission, the patient may have been given an initial diagnosis or a rule-out diagnosis. At the time of treatment planning, a substantiated diagnosis must be recorded. It may be the same as the initial diagnosis, or, based on new information and assessment, it may differ. Rule-out diagnoses, by themselves are not acceptable as a substantiated diagnosis. Data to substantiate the diagnosis may be found in, but is not limited to, the psychiatric evaluation, the medical history and physical examination, laboratory tests, medical and other psychological consults, assessments done by disciplines involved in patient evaluations and information supplied from other sources such as community agencies and significant others. §482.61(c)(1)(i) PROBES What specific problems will be treated during the patient's hospitalization? Does the treatment plan identify and precisely describe problem behaviors rather than generalized statements i.e., "paranoid," "aggressive," "depressed?" or generic terminology i.e., "alteration in thought process," "ineffective coping," "alteration in mood?" Are physical problems identified and included in the treatment plan if they require treatment, or interfere with treatment, during the patient's hospitalization?
B121	(ii) Short-term and long range goals;	§482.61(c)(1)(ii) GUIDANCE: Based on the problems identified for treatment, short-term and long range goals are developed. Whether the use of short-term or a combination of short-term and long range goals is appropriate is dependent on the length of hospital stay.

| B121 (continued) | | Short-term and long range goals include specific dates for expected achievement. As goals are achieved, the treatment plan should be revised. When a goal is modified, changed or discontinued without achievement, the plan should be reviewed for relevancy, and updated as needed.

In crisis intervention and short-term treatment there may be only one timeframe for treatment goals. As the length of hospital stay increases (often because of the long-term chronic nature of the patient's illness), both long range and short-term goals are needed.

The long range goal is achieved through the development of a series of short-term goals, i.e., smaller, logical sequential steps which will result in reaching the long range goal. Both the short-term and long range goals must be stated as expected behavioral outcomes for the patient. Goals must be related to the problems identified for treatment. Goals must be written as observable, measurable patient behaviors to be achieved. Discharge criteria may be included as long range goals.

§482.61(c)(1)(ii) PROBES:

How do treatment plan goals relate to the problems being treated?

Do goals indicate the outcomes to be achieved by the patient?

Are the goals written in a way that allow changes in the patient's behavior to be measured?

If not apparent, what criteria do staff use to measure success?

How relevant are the treatment plan goals to the patient's condition? |
| B122 | (iii) The specific treatment modalities utilized; | §482.61(c)(1)(iii) GUIDANCE:

This requirement refers to all of the planned treatment modalities used to treat the patient during hospitalization. Having identified the problems requiring treatment, and defining outcome goals to be achieved, appropriate treatment approaches must be identified.

Modalities include all of the active treatment measures provided to the patient. It describes the treatment which will be provided to the patient. It describes the treatment which will be provided by various staff.

A daily schedule of unit activities does not, in itself, constitute planned modalities of treatment. It is expected that when a patient attends various |

B122
(continued)

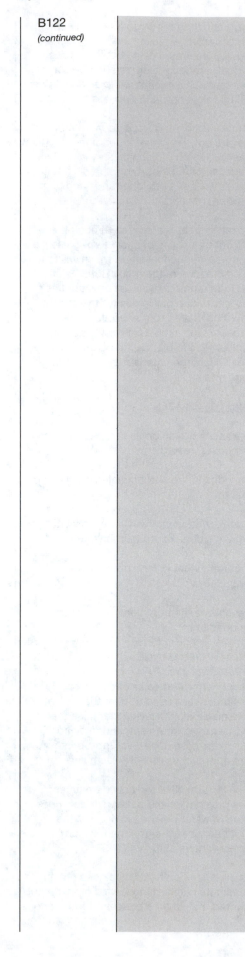

treatment modalities/activities, it is a part of individualized planning with a specific purpose and focus for that patient.

Simply "naming" modalities (i.e., individual therapy, group therapy, occupational therapy, medication education) is not acceptable. The focus of the treatment must be included.

Simply "stating" modality approaches (i.e., "set limits," "encourage socialization," "discharge planning as needed") is not acceptable. Modality approaches must be specifically described in order to assure consistency of approach.

Observation of staff implementing treatment, both in structured and non-structured settings, is a major criterion to determine whether active treatment is being provided in accordance with planned treatment.

It must be clear to you that the active treatment received by the patient is internally consistent and not simply a series of disconnected specific modalities delivered within certain scheduled intervals.

§482.61(c)(1)(iii) PROBES:

Are qualified staff observed following the methods, approaches and staff intervention as stated?

Can staff explain the focus of the modality they have provided?

Are observed treatment methods, approaches and interventions from all disciplines included in the plan?

Do the pieces of the treatment plan work together to achieve the greatest possible gain for the patient?

Does the hospital integrate its activities, therapies, treatments, and patient routines to work for the patient's therapeutic interests first, and its own convenience second?

Do the disciplines present at observed treatment planning meetings represent all of the patient's needs?

If the patient attends treatment planning, how do the staff prepare the patient to participate?

If the patient does not attend, what reasons do staff give to explain the absence?

Is there a process to enable staff to reach a consensus regarding how treatment will be carried out?

B122 *(continued)*		Is the patient included in the decision-making, whenever possible? Are the final decisions regarding treatment approaches defined clearly by the end of the discussion? How does the patient get to know his/her treatment regime? How does the treatment team encourage the patient to accept responsibility for engaging in the treatment regime, rather than accepting it passively?
B123	(iv) The responsibilities of each member of the treatment team;	§482.61(c)(1)(iv) GUIDANCE: There are no "correct" number of staff who comprise the treatment team. The disciplines involved in the patient's treatment depend upon the problems to be treated, the short-term and long range goals and the treatment approaches and modalities used to achieve the goals. The intent of the regulation is to insure that each individual on the treatment team who is primarily responsible for ensuring compliance with particular aspects of the patient's individualized treatment program is identified. Identification of the staff should be recorded in a manner that includes the name and discipline of the individual. If other professionals or paraprofessionals provide care, the facility has the latitude to decide the manner with which it will identify them on the treatment plan. The patient, as well as family/significant others, should be aware of the staff responsible for various aspects of treatment. §482.61(c)(1)(iv) PROBES: Are staff who are designated in the treatment plan observed carrying out treatment activities and therapies? Is the information in the plan consistent with surveyor observations? Are the patients able to name the staff responsible for implementing their treatment? Is this information consistent with the treatment plan?
	and	
B124	(v)Adequate documentation to justify the diagnosis and the treatment and rehabilitation activities carried out.	§482.61(c)(1)(v) GUIDANCE: When the progress and treatment notes are When the progress and treatment notes are reviewed, the content of the notes must relate to the treatment plan. The notes must indicate what the hospital staff is doing to carry out the treatment plan and the patient's response to the interventions.

B124 *(continued)*		<u>§482.61(c)(1)(v) PROBES:</u> Are the treatment notes relative to the identified problems? Are the treatment notes indicative of the patient's response to treatment? Do the progress notes relate to specific patient problems or progress?
B125	(2) The treatment received by the patient must be documented in such a way to assure that all active therapeutic efforts are included.	§482.61(c)(2) GUIDANCE: Active treatment is an essential requirement for inpatient psychiatric care. Active treatment is a clinical process involving ongoing assessment, diagnosis, intervention, evaluation of care and treatment, and planning for discharge and aftercare, under the direction of a psychiatrist. The patient is in the hospital because it has been determined that the patient requires intensive, 24 hour, specialized psychiatric intervention that cannot be provided outside the psychiatric hospital. The medical record must indicate that the hospital adheres to the patient's right to be counseled about medication, its intended effects, and the potential side-effects. If the patient requires, because of danger to self or others, a more restrictive environment, the hospital must indicate that the staff attempted to care for the patient in the least restrictive setting before progressing to a more restrictive setting. Through observation, look for evidence that each patient is receiving all the aspects of treatment to which the hospital has committed itself based upon his/her assessment, evaluation and plan of care. It is the hospital's responsibility to provide those treatment modalities with sufficient frequency and intensity to assure that the patient achieves his/her optimal level of functioning. Through observation and interviews, look for evidence that each patient's rights are being addressed and protected. There should be policies and procedures in place to address the following areas: informed consent, confidentiality, privacy, and security. Expect to see detailed policies and procedures regarding the therapeutic use of restrictions, such as visitors, mail, and phone calls. Seclusion and restraint policies and procedures must address patient protection and safety while in a restricted setting. <u>Clarification of the types of notes found in the medical record.</u> **Treatment notes** are recordings in the medical record that indicate provision of, and a patient's response to, a specific modality. This modality may be drug therapy, individual, family, marital, or

B125
(continued)

group therapy, art therapy, recreational therapy, and any specialized therapy ordered by the physician or anyone credentialed by the facility, in accordance with the State law, to write orders in the medical record.

A combined treatment and progress note may be written.

Progress notes are recordings in the medical record that are written by persons directly responsible for the care and active treatment of the patient. Progress notes give a chronological picture of how the patient is progressing toward the accomplishment of the individual goals in the treatment plan. These are frequently shift notes, weekly notes, or monthly notes.

§482.61(c)(2) PROBES:

Does the patient know his/her diagnosis?

What did the patient contribute to the formulation of the treatment plan? Goals of treatment?

If the patient receives medication, does the patient understand the reason for the medication? The name of the medication? The dose prescribed? The time of administration? The desired effects? The potential side-effects?

If medication is changed, is there a rationale for the change?

Are staff members recording their observations relative to the patient's response to the treatment modalities, including medication?

Is there evidence that the patient was afforded the opportunity to participate in his/her plan of care?

What progress has the patient made? Has the patient achieved his/her optimal level of functioning? If not, why? Are these reasons/barriers reflected in the current treatment plan? Do treatment and progress notes support these insights?

Does the observed status of the patient in the various treatment modalities correspond to the progress note reports of status?

Do all treatment team members document their observations and interventions so that the information is available to the entire team?

If a restrictive procedure is used (e.g., restraint and/or seclusion), is there evidence that attempts were made systematically to treat the patient in the least restrictive manner?

B125 (continued)		Is there evidence that the rights of the patient were protected while in the restrictive setting in accordance with Federal and State law and accepted standards of practice?
	(d) Standard: Recording Progress	
B126	Progress notes must be recorded by the doctor of medicine or osteopathy responsible for the care of the patient as specified in §482.12(c),	§482.61(d) GUIDANCE: Refer to §482.61(c)(2) GUIDANCE for clarification between treatment notes and progress notes. The recording of progress is evidence of individual patient performance. Specifically, the progress notes recorded by the professional staff, or others responsible for the patient's treatment, must give a chronological picture of the patient's progress or lack of progress towards attaining short and long range goals outlined in the individual treatment plan. Progress notes should relate to the goals of the treatment plan. Notes that state, "patient slept well" or "no complaints" constitute observations and do not indicate how the patient is responding to treatment and progressing towards set goals. Frequency alone does not determine the adequacy of progress notes. Expect to see greater frequency when patients are more acutely ill and/or in a crisis of some kind. Notes should be dated and signed (signature and title or discipline). §482.61(d) PROBES: Are the physicians who are significantly involved in active treatment modalities/interventions actually documenting progress? Do the progress notes relate to the goals of the treatment plan? Do they include precise statements of progress? Is there a correlation between what is observed by the surveyor and what is described in the notes? Do the notes give a clear picture of the patient's progress or lack thereof, during the course of hospitalization? In reviewing the patient's progress, are aftercare/discharge plans being evaluated?
B127	nurse,	§482.61(d) PROBES: Are the nurses who are significantly involved in active treatment modalities/interventions actually documenting progress?

B128	social worker	§482.61(d) PROBES: Are the social workers who are significantly involved in active treatment modalities/interventions plan actually documenting progress?
B129	when appropriate, others significantly involved in active treatment modalities.	§482.61(d) PROBES: Are staff from other disciplines, i.e., rehabilitative therapy and psychology, who are significantly involved in active treatment modalities/ interventions actually documenting progress?
B130	The frequency of progress notes is determined by the condition of the patient but must be recorded at least weekly for the first 2 months and at least once a month thereafter,	§482.61(d) PROBES: What is the frequency of progress notes in relation to the condition of the patient?
	and must contain	
B131	recommendations for revisions in the treatment plan as indicated	§482.61(d) PROBES: Do the progress notes contain documentation substantiating changes/revisions in the treatment plan and subsequent assessment of the patient's responses and progress
	as well as	
B132	a precise assessment of the patient's progress in accordance with the original or revised treatment plan.	§482.61(d) PROBES: Do the notes give a clear picture of the patient's progress, or lack thereof, during the course of hospitalization? Are the progress notes related to the goals of the treatment plan?
	(e) Standard: Discharge planning and discharge summary	
B133	The record of each patient who has been discharged must have a discharge summary that includes a recapitulation of the patient's hospitalization	§482.61(e) GUIDANCE: The record of each patient who has been discharged should indicate the extent to which goals established in the patient's treatment plan have been met. As part of discharge planning, staff consider the discharge alternatives addressed in the psychosocial assessment and the extent to which the goals in the treatment plan have been met. The surveyor should refer to hospital policy for discharge timeframes.

B133 *(continued)*		The discharge summary should contain a recapitulation of the patient's hospitalization, which is a summary of the circumstances and rationale for admission, and a synopsis of accomplishments achieved as reflected through the treatment plan. This summary includes the reasons for admission, treatment achieved during hospitalization, a baseline of the psychiatric, physical and social functioning of the patient at the time of discharge, and evidence of the patient/family response to the treatment interventions.
	and	
B134	recommendations from appropriate services concerning follow-up or aftercare	§482.61(e) GUIDANCE: The patient's discharge summary should describe the services and supports that are appropriate to the patient's needs and that will be effective on the day of discharge. Examples include: • A complete description of arrangements with treatment and other community resources for the provision of follow-up services. Reference should be made to prior verbal and written communication and exchange of information; • A plan outlining psychiatric, medical/physical treatment and the medication regimen as applicable; • Specific appointment date(s) and names and addresses of the service provider(s); • Description of community housing/living arrangement; • Economic/financial status or plan, i.e., supplemental security income benefits; • Recreational and leisure resources; and • A complete description of the involvement of family and significant others with the patient after discharge. §482.61(e) PROBES: How does the discharge planning process verify appointment source(s), dates and addresses? How was the patient involved in the discharge and aftercare planning process? Were discharge related documents made available to the patient, family, community treatment source and/or any other appropriate sources? Is there indication that the discharge planning process included the participation of multi-disciplinary staff and the patient? Have the results been communicated to the post-hospital treatment entity?

B134 *(continued)*		Is there evidence that contact with the post-hospital treatment entity included communication of treatment recommendations (including information regarding the patient's medications)? Is a contact person named, and does the patient have a specific appointment date and time for the initial follow-up visit?
	as well as	
B135	a brief summary of the patient's condition on discharge.	§482.61(e) GUIDANCE: The patient's discharge planning process should address anticipated problems after discharge and suggested means for intervention, i.e., accessibility and availability of community resources and support systems including transportation, special problems related to the patient's functional ability to participate in aftercare planning. The discharge summary and/or plan should contain information about the status of the patient on the day of discharge, including psychiatric, physical and functional condition.

Appendix B:
Self-Test
Answers

CHAPTER 1 ANSWERS

1. What causes patients to seek mental health care?

   People seek treatment when they become overwhelmed and lack the capacity to deal with their problems.

2. What is a treatment plan?

   A treatment plan is a therapeutic roadmap to recovery. In its simplest form, this plan will help the patient resolve enough problems so that he or she can function at a higher level and move to a less restrictive treatment environment.

3. What are the five principles of successful treatment planning?

   - *The patient should know what problems the treatment plan will address.*
   - *The patient should know who his or her therapist is and how the therapist plans to help resolve his or her problems.*
   - *The patient should know what treatment modalities (i.e., medications, group therapy, activities therapy, family therapy, etc.) will be utilized to deal with the problems, and how often he or she will be expected to participate in these forms of treatment.*
   - *The patient should understand the expected outcomes of his or her treatment.*
   - *The patient and the treatment team must both understand and participate in the formulation and implementation of the patient's individualized treatment plan.*

4. Who is responsible for formulating a treatment plan?

   The patient and the treatment team must both understand and participate in the formulation and implementation of the patient's individualized treatment plan.

5. Define a continuum of care.

The continuum of care is the process of managing patients in a progressive range of treatment environments, depending on the severity of the patients' problems.

CHAPTER 2 ANSWERS

1. What does the term *insurance coverage* mean?

   Insurance coverage delineates the scope of services that will be reimbursed, and the amount of money that will be paid for those services.

2. What are three conditions of participation in the Medicare psychiatric program?

   1. *The treatment facility must meet special staffing standards.*
   2. *The treatment facility must comply with special conditions for managing their medical records.*
      - *This standard of care primarily deals with treatment planning. The guidelines governing treatment plans are extremely specific.*
   3. *The treatment facility must comply with stringent discharge planning criteria.*
      - *CMS introduced this condition of participation in 1995. They recognized that hospital stays were getting shorter and that preparing a patient to move to another level of care was a critical piece of the plan for care.*

3. What are two common perceptions of mental health treatment that led to managed care?

   1. *Psychiatric and drug abuse patients stayed in the hospital until their benefits (coverage) ran out.*
   2. *Although psychiatric patients stayed in hospitals for months and insurance companies funded tens of millions of dollars for psychiatric care, the patients did not get well.*

4. Who usually shares the cost of employee health benefits?

   Employees and employers share the cost of health care insurance.

5. What does CMS stand for and what is its role in health care?

   The Center for Medicare and Medicaid Services, or CMS, is the agency of the U.S. government that oversees the payment for and quality of the Medicare and Medicaid Programs.

6. What does JCAHO stand for?

   The Joint Commission on Accreditation of Health Care Organizations.

CHAPTER 3 ANSWERS

1. What are two reasons therapists historically give for not completing treatment plans?

    1. *"Treatment plans are just something we have to write to make the surveyors happy. We really do not use them for anything."*
    2. *"If therapists spent all their time writing treatment plans, there would not be any time left to take care of the patient."*

2. What are the two reasons Walt Disney believed people failed?

    1. *People do not understand what they are expected to do.*
    2. *People do not have the resources to accomplish their tasks.*

3. CMS requires staff to specify four distinct parts for every intervention on the treatment plan. Name them.

    1. *The patient will know the name and discipline of the member of the treatment team who is primarily responsible for seeing that the intervention is completed.*
    2. *The patient will understand what treatment modality the team will use to address each problem.*
    3. *The patient will know the focus of each therapy he or she attends? He or she will understand the purpose for attending that specific treatment modality.*
    4. *The patient will know the frequency of the treatment interventions or modalities (how often he or she will attend).*

4. What are two benefits of good treatment planning for a facility?

    1. *Better care leads to a better reputation.*
    2. *Better documentation leads to financial soundness.*

CHAPTER 4 ANSWERS

1. What are diagnostic criteria?

    The DSM-IV-TR simply tries to give a description of the clinical symptomology and does not depend on any theoretical framework or school of therapy. These descriptions of clinical symptomology are diagnostic criteria.

2. What is a multiaxial diagnosis and why is it useful in treating mental disorders?

    According to the DSM-IV-TR, there are five axes for listing a patient's diagnosis. Each axis deals with a different physical or developmental aspect of the diagnosis.

3. What does the fifth digit of a diagnostic code denote?

    The fifth digit is used to denote the current state of the disorder.

4. What types of disorders belong on the following axes?

- *Axis I—Clinical Disorders and V-Codes*
- *Axis II—Behavioral Disorders and Mental Retardation*
- *Axis III—Medical Diagnosis*
- *Axis IV—Psychosocial Stressors*
- *Axis V—GAF Scale*

5. What is a V-Code? On what axis do you record it?

A V-Code is a relational problem. Although the problem is not a psychiatric disorder, it is intrusive enough to warrant primary attention during treatment. It is recorded on Axis I.

CHAPTER 5 ANSWERS

1. What are the two main objectives of assessments?

Assessments are used to gather the information mecessary to substantiate a diagnosis and to ensure successful treatment.

2. How long does CMS allow the treatment team to use a provisional or rule out diagnosis?

CMS allows for the temporary use of unsubstantiated diagnosis for up to 72 hours.

3. Define the following terms:

- *Admission diagnosis—When a patient is admitted to treatment he or she is required to have a diagnosis. The admission diagnosis derives from a brief intake assessment and clinical history.*
- *Provisional diagnosis—A provisional diagnosis is used when it is believed that the diagnosis will ultimately be met and there is inadequate information available for a firm diagnosis at the present time.*
- *Rule-out diagnosis—A rule-out diagnosis is used when a diagnostician suspects the patient has a certain diagnosis but wants to rule out other etiologies or causes before giving a substantiated diagnosis.*
- *Substantiated diagnosis—A substantiated diagnosis is the diagnosis identified by the treatment team to be the primary focus upon which treatment planning will be based. It evolves from the synthesis of data from the various disciplines.*

4. What does the term *multidisciplinary treatment team* mean?

A multidisciplinary team is a term used to describe a treatment team comprised of various clinical disciplines who use their combined clinical insights to treat the patient.

5. What is the minimum number of treatment team members, and what disciplines must they represent?

The number and types of disciplines represented on the treatment team will vary based on the types of problems to be treated. At a minimum, a treatment team will always have a physician and a nurse.

CHAPTER 6 ANSWERS

1. What are the two main objectives of assessments?

    1. *Substantiating the diagnosis and*
    2. *Discovering what the patient's strengths are, and drawing on them to help the patient gain insight into his or her problems.*

2. What is another interchangeable term for a patient's assets?

    Patient's strengths is another term for patient's assets

3. Define the term *biopsychosocial.*

    - *Biological = Medical or physiological problems*
    - *Psychological = Problems with personality, feelings, thoughts, or intellect*
    - *Sociological = Environmental and social problems to include family*

4. How many disciplines must be represented on the treatment team?

    Although there is no set number of treatment team members, the number of members should be related to the length of stay and the complexity of the problems present. At a minimum, the team will have a nurse and a physician.

5. List the seven major assessments, the disciplines responsible for providing them, and the time frame to complete the assessments.

    a. *Nursing—Nursing Service—8 hours*
    b. *H&P—Physician—24 hours*
    c. *Psychiatric Evaluation—Psychiatrist—60 hours*
    d. *Psychosocial Evaluation—Social Worker—72 hours*
    e. *Leisure Skills Assessment—OT, CODA, RT—72 hours*
    f. *Dietary—RD-72 Hours*
    g. *Psychological—Psychologist—72 Hours*

CHAPTER 7 ANSWERS

1. What is a problem statement?

    "A disability is any psychiatric, biopsychosocial problem requiring treatment intervention." ☞ B119 *The terms* disability *and* problem *are interchangeable, so a problem statement is any problem that requires treatment.*

2. What is Johnson's rule?

    A diagnosis can never be a problem statement, except Axis III diagnoses which are always problems.

3. Can a nursing diagnosis be used as a problem statement? Explain your answer.

    Absolutely not, nursing diagnoses are too vague to be considered as problem statements.

4. What is the difference between a diagnosis, a psychiatric criterion, and a problem statement?

    Clusters of criteria define a diagnosis; each diagnosis has a specific set of criteria that define the disorder. Problem statements are specific behaviors that may or may not be criteria in themselves.

5. What does it mean when a treatment team cannot find problems related to the diagnostic criteria?

    The treatment team has the wrong diagnosis.

6. List three problem statements related to the diagnostic criteria of depressed mood.

    1. Sadness

    2. Feelings of hopelessness

    3. Tearfulness

    Of course, there are others! (See page 48.)

7. What is a manifestation and how does is make a difference in the patient's treatment regimen?

    Manifestations describe and document how a problem manifests itself in a particular patient. In other words, "what does this behavior look like in my patient?"

8. What is the key to problem resolution?

    The key to problem resolution is clarity. Once you have defined the appropriate problem and described its manifestations correctly, it is easy to move forward in treatment.

CHAPTER 8 ANSWERS

1. What is a long-term goal?

    A measurable, objective indicator that shows that the patient/client, family, or caregiver has acquired enough skills/tools to be ready/safe for discharge.

2. What is a short-term goal?

    A short-term goal defines and measures the intermediate steps the patient must take to achieve the treatment plan goal for discharge.

3. What are three reasons for having short-term goals?

    a. *Create measurement of the success or failure of treatment intervention.*

    b. *A time frame for treatment interventions. CMS requires that all goals are time limited, and dating goals places a time expectation on completion of treatment.*

    c. *Quick, achievable objectives build the patient's confidence in his or her ability to succeed in therapy. Success increases his or her self-belief that the treatment team can help him or her get better.*

4. What does the therapist/team define as long-term goals?

    Long-term goals may be planned for post-discharge; treatment in all settings should limit long-term goals to a point in treatment that the therapist/treatment team feels good about discharging the patient and moving him or her along the continuum of care.

5. What are the four possible treatment outcomes for long-term goals?

   a. *The problem is resolved.*

   b. *The problem has improved.*

   c. *The patient has gained insight without making progress.*

   d. *Arrangements for continued treatment will have to be made so that therapy can continue in the next level of care.*

CHAPTER 9 ANSWERS

1. Why delineate interventions?

   Interventions describe what the staff is going to do to help the patient achieve his or her goals. Increased specificity will increase understanding and compliance.

2. What are the four areas of specificity in a good intervention?

   a. *Person responsible*

   b. *Modality*

   c. *Focus*

   d. *Frequency*

3. Who benefits from good interventions?

   The patient and the staff benefit from good interventions. Good interventions define their roles and responsibilities in recovery.

4. Why is it important to name the person responsible for ensuring the intervention is completed?

   Someone has to be responsible for seeing that the patient receives good treatment. If everyone is responsible, no one is responsible.

5. Why should a licensed person be careful when delegating the day-to-day function of an intervention?

   When a licensed individual is responsible for monitoring nonlicensed staff, the nonlicensed staff works on the authority of the licensed staff member. If something goes wrong, it is his or her license that is in jeopardy.

CHAPTER 10 ANSWERS

1. How do we measure a patient's progress toward treatment goals?

   By constantly monitoring and documenting the patient's progress and changing the plan when the patient completes goals or fails to make progress toward recovery.

2. How often are you required to have a treatment team update meeting?

   There is no requirement related to how often a treatment team update meeting must be held.

3. What are the required parts of a progress note?

   • *Date*

   • *Time*

   • *Problem number*

   It is also essential that each note be signed and list the discipline of the individual who wrote the note.

4. What is the purpose of a treatment team signature sheet?

    A treatment plan signature sheet authenticates the time and date of treatment team meetings. They further document participants in the meeting and the role the patient or designee played in developing the plan.

5   What old treatment axiom is Surveyor Rule Number One?

    If it is not documented, it has not been done.

6. How would you define *active treatment*?

    Active treatment is an essential requirement for inpatient psychiatric care. Active treatment is a clinical process involving the ongoing assessment, diagnosis, intervention, evaluation of care, and treatment and planning under the direction of a psychiatrist.

7. What patient situations would necessitate a treatment team update meeting?
    *   *The patient achieves a goal.*
    *   *The patient fails to make progress toward a goal.*
    *   *A new problem is identified.*
    *   *A problem is dropped from the treatment plan.*

CHAPTER 11 ANSWERS

1. What do the letters A, B, and C stand for in the ABC model of treatment?

    A—Assessment
    B—Band-Aid blockages
    C—Continue the care in a less restrictive environment

2. What is the number one reason for readmission to psychiatric treatment?

    The patient's noncompliance to the plan of care. Specifically, the patient's noncompliance with taking medications.

3. Name two advantages to moving a patient into a lower level of care.
    1. *The patient is able to function in a less restrictive environment (one more closely approximating his or her home).*
    2. *It costs less to treat patients in a lower level of intensity.*

4. What is the purpose of a continuum of care?

    A continuum of care is necessary to provide patients with lower, less intense treatment environments that continue to protect them in a less restrictive and more home-like fashion.

5. What is the only real chance a patient has to succeed when he or she moves to a less restrictive environment?

    Good discharge planning is the key. For a patient to succeed, the plan must be laid for the continuation of a protective environment in a lower level of care.

6. What is the primary purpose of the summary in the discharge plan?

    The purpose of the summary is to provide the therapist in the next level of care with insight into the already completed treatment process. It also allows the therapist to build upon an existing plan of care without starting treatment over.

CHAPTER 12 ANSWERS

1. What is an acuity scale?

   An acuity scale is a means of measuring the severity of problems manifested by the patients in treatment.

2. What is the primary disadvantage to rating patient progress using subjective ordinate scales?

   Each patient is rated according to his or her single circumstances and there is no connectivity between patients and the ability for universal interpretation of the treatment data or progress. Simply put, a subjective ordinal scale is only meaningful to the patient and therapist for whom it was designed. It cannot be used as a basis to rate multiple patients with varied symptomology.

3. What are the six stages of recovery?

   - *Protect*
   - *Stabilize*
   - *Motivate*
   - *Direct*
   - *Educate*
   - *Reintegrate*

4. What is a discharge screen?

   A discharge screen is a test that is applied to a specific problem to see if a blockage remains that would keep the patient from leaving the hospital.

5. At what point on the Patient Severity Scale should the team begin to monitor the continued use of inpatient treatment?

   When the patient is rated at five or below on the patient severity scale. Many insurance companies would insist that the patient be discharged when he or she no longer met the criteria for commitment.

CHAPTER 13 ANSWERS

1. What does "perception is reality" mean?

   The "truth" is not an absolute term. Perceptions color a person's opinions and this colored perception is very real to that person. Hence, perception becomes reality.

2. What are three reasons that outcomes measurement has been elusive?

   1. Everyone has a different expectation of treatment success.
   2. Nobody wants to be accountable for results.
   3. Patients with different diagnoses all look and act differently.

3. What is the purpose of a utilization review grid?

   The purpose of a utilization review grid index is to match the intensity of the problem with the intensity of the treatment to allow the treatment team to acquire a full representation of the patient's problem.

4. What is meant by the term *biopsychosocial*?

    Let's begin by looking at the term biopsychosocial *and refine the types of problems described.*

    - *Biological = Medical or physiological problems. These issues are physical or chemical in nature and constitute the highest degree of severity*
    - *Psychological = Problems with personality, feelings, thoughts, or intellect*
    - *Sociological = Environmental and social problems to include: family, drug-related lifestyles, employment, and whether the patient can safely return to his or her environment*

5. What are the staff tasks (focii) of treatment in the order that the patient receives them?

    1. *Protect and stabilize.*
    2. *Motivate the patient to want to get better.*
    3. *Direct the patient's therapeutic process.*
    4. *Educate the patient about his or her disease and recovery skills.*
    5. *Reintegrate the patient into the next environment using good discharge planning.*

CHAPTER 15 ANSWERS

1. What circumstances would most likely prompt a surveyor to ask for an initial treatment plan?

    The reason surveyors request an initial plan of care is to justify active treatment.

2. What is the purpose of an initial treatment plan?

    The surveyors want to make sure that the first three days of treatment are not wasted days.

    The surveyors want to make sure that the patient is receiving active treatment for the payment received. Remember that CMS wants to ensure they are getting what they paid for.

    Finally, and most importantly, the surveyors want to make sure that the staff is protecting the patient.

3. What is meant by the term *active treatment*?

    Active treatment is an essential requirement for inpatient psychiatric care. Active treatment is a clinical process involving the ongoing assessment, diagnosis, intervention, evaluation of care and treatment, and planning under the direction of a psychiatrist.

4. What is Surveyor Rule Number Two?

    Do not argue with a surveyor; it is not productive and you will not win.

5. What is the difference between writing interventions for initial care plans and the master treatment plan?

    Since the plan's purpose is to protect or stabilize the patient, the long-term and short-term goals for an initial plan of care will be reduced to a checklist and there is not a manifestation statement.

Glossary

accreditation A survey process used to determine that a facility meets or exceeds the standards set forth by the accrediting body.

active treatment A clinical process involving the ongoing assessment, diagnosis, intervention, and evaluation of care and treatment and planning under the direction of a psychiatrist.

acuity scale A system of measurement that determines the severity of a patient's behavioral problems as well as the intensity of staff interventions necessary to manage the patient.

admission diagnosis A type of diagnosis used to admit patients to a treatment setting or hospital. Typically the admitting physician will use an admission diagnosis when there is either not enough information available on admission or the admitting clinician derives his or her diagnostic information from the intake assessment and plans to substantiate diagnostic information at a later date.

AOA American Osteopathic Association.

assessments A discipline-specific tool used to evaluate a patient.

attestation statement A CMS form that is sent to providers on a yearly basis to attest to the fact that they are following the CMS special conditions of participation. The forms are signed by the CEO and have the force of law.

baseline Specific rate or occurrence of a particular behavior as recorded during a period before interventions are begun.

B. I. D. Bis in die (Latin for "twice a day," prescription dosage).

biopsychosocial A term coined to frame the focus of a patient's particular problem.

blockage A term that refers to any problem that prevents the patient's progress into the next level of the continuum of care.

bylaws A set of rules and regulations used by hospitals to set out and delineate the way their medical or professional staff will operate.

canned plan A treatment plan that provides the same level of care and interventions to all patients regardless of their specific problems. A system of treating patients that ignores individualized needs in favor of a systematic approach, where all patients receive the same treatment material and interventions.

carve-out When an insurance provider chooses to separate the management and funding for mental health benefits or other types of special care.

case management The assignment of a mental health provider to assist the patient to make sure health care and social services provide required services.

chronic mental patient An individual who has had long-term psychiatric hospitalization within the past 5 years, or two or more psychiatric hospitalizations within the past 12 months.

close observation In a behavioral health setting this term refers to the need for insuring the patient's continued safety by face to face observation at all times. It is a step down in intensity from one to one observation.

CMS Center for Medicare and Medicaid Services An agency of the U.S. government charged with the management of the Medicare and Medicaid programs. Formerly known as The Health Care Financing Administration or HCFA.

cognitive therapy Therapies that deal with knowing and understanding. Emphasis is placed on learning rules, strategies, and principles.

commitment Involuntary admission to a psychiatric hospital. Patients are afforded *legal involuntary* protection because they are a danger to themselves or others or are unable to carry out activities of daily living.

community mental health center A community-based treatment agency that provides a social model of psychiatric care and promotes a wide range of services within the community.

continuum of care A group of interrelated treatment settings or levels of care designed to return a patient to the least restrictive treatment atmosphere as his or her condition improves.

coping skills Any skill set directed at managing stressors. A technique designed to reduce emotional distress.

deemed status When a hospital is accredited by the AOA or JCAHO, it is "deemed" to meet the standards established for participation in the Medicare program, except for psychiatric services. Psychiatric services are required to meet the additional, special conditions of participation.

deescalation techniques Therapeutic techniques employed by staff/therapists and/or taught to patients to reduce the level of agitative, dangerous, or acting-out behavior exhibited by clients/patients in various treatment settings.

depression An abnormally long period of feelings of hopelessness, sadness, or grief.

detoxification The medical or social function of removing toxins (alcohol or drugs) from a client's system. When medical detoxification occurs, the practitioner usually substitutes an alternative medication to help manage the gradual withdrawal process.

diagnosis The act or process of identifying behavioral or medical criteria that define the structure of a disease through examinations and assessments.

diagnostic criteria A series of behaviors, groups of behaviors, or problems that are used to substantiate a diagnosis.

disability Any biopsychosocial problem requiring treatment intervention. The terms disability and problem are used interchangeably.

discharge The patient is released from the hospital or current level of care.

discharge planning A clinical report that recapitulates the patient's progress (or lack of progress) in treatment and outlines the plan for transitioning the patient from one level of mental health care or environmental setting to another.

discharge screen A test that is applied to a specific problem to see if a blockage remains that would keep the patient in the current level of care.

DSM-IV-TR The current version of the *Diagnostic and Statistical Manual*, which provides specific guidelines and diagnostic criteria for various mental and psychiatric disorders.

elopement A term used to describe the escape of any patient who is restricted to the unit or facility for legal or safety reasons.

estimated length of stay The period of time the attending psychiatrist or treating professional anticipates the patient will be in the hospital.

ethic A standard or valued behavior adhered to by an individual or group.

expressive therapies Therapy geared to assisting the client to express conflict and anxiety through a series of different mediums, including but not limited to art, music, dialogue, and role-playing.

family therapy Treatment of the family unit as a social system rather than focusing the therapy on the specific patient.

fast track A term used to describe the letter sent to a facility that has failed a CMS survey. A fast track letter or notification could lead to removal from participation in the Medicare Program within 28 days unless the survey deficiencies are corrected.

focus of treatment The means a treatment team uses to help a patient manage specific problems.

GAF scale The Global Assessment of Functioning scale is a measurement tool found in the *DSM* to help a therapist pinpoint and define the patient's level of functioning.

geriatric patient A patient who receives physical or mental health services and is over the age of 65.

group therapy A therapeutic process or setting that usually involves a limited number of patients (6–8) that is conducted by a therapist for the purpose of discussing and working on a variety of common therapy issues.

guidance An explanatory section in the Medicare standards regarding the survey standards.

hallucinations A sensory experience involving hearing, seeing, feeling, smelling, or tasting that is not due to external stimuli.

HCFA See CMS.

HMO Health Maintenance Organization; a type of managed care.

hopelessness An expression of patient belief that neither he or she nor anyone else can do anything to change his or her current situation.

individual therapy A one-on-one therapeutic relationship that encourages the patient to explore and develop insights into relationships, thoughts, feelings, and behavior.

individualized treatment Treating each patient with individual interventions customized to meet his or her needs as opposed to using a "canned" program approach. *See* Canned Plan.

intensity of treatment The level of care currently being provided by the therapist or treatment staff.

interventions A section of the treatment plan that specifically outlines what the staff will do for the patient to help resolve his or her problems.

isolation Splitting off the emotional process of thought; removing oneself from the social process.

JCAHO The Joint Commission on Accreditation of Health Care Organizations. A voluntary accrediting body that manages a series of survey processes in various healthcare settings to ensure quality of care.

least restrictive environment Providing patient care in the environment that provides the greatest freedom from restriction, especially a long-term psychiatric hospitalization.

long-term goal A written statement outlining a measurable, objective indicator that shows that the patient/client, family, or caregiver has acquired enough skills and tools to be ready and safe for discharge. In some cases, long-term goals may be written as discharge criteria.

manifestations A behaviorally written description of a particular problem that allows the treatment team to further clarify the associated behaviors.

mental status exam An evaluation of the patient's functioning concerning sensory processes, thinking, judgment, mood, affect, and insight.

milieu A term used to describe the patient's therapeutic environment.

milieu therapy Manipulation of the patient's environment to produce a desired therapeutic result.

modalities The therapeutic format (group therapy, individual therapy, recreational therapy, etc.) used by a therapist or treatment team to deal with a problem.

multidisciplinary treatment team A group of health care therapists from various disciplines who work as a team to treat the client from their own discipline-specific set of services.

noncompliance The failure of a patient/client to carry out a preordained plan of mental health care.

nursing diagnosis The independent judgment of a nurse of the patient's behavioral response to stress.

orienting patient This term can have two meanings. **Orienting to the unit or setting** means that a new patient is shown the unit or therapeutic setting and introduced to the staff and other patients. The rules of the therapeutic setting are explained to the patient. **Orienting to reality** is assessing the patient's ability to correctly recognize and identify a number of predetermined indicators, such as time, place, and date, in order to establish their level of functioning.

outcomes (treatment) A measurement of the success of mental health treatment.

out-of-pocket The amount of money required to pay the bill after insurance has paid its portion; or, if the patient or client has no insurance, the entire amount of the bill.

peruse An intense scrutiny of a particular document for information.

physical restraint Immobilizing the patient physically by use of mechanical means or by limiting or confining a person to a specific area.

problem *See* Disability.

progress notes A statement recorded in the patient's/client's medical record or chart that is used to document the patient's response to the treatment interventions provided by the therapist or treatment team.

provisional diagnosis A diagnosis used to begin treatment, when the clinician expects that the full criteria for the diagnosis will ultimately be met.

psychomotor retardation A slowing of the motor response, generally in response to depression.

reality orientation The process of orienting patients so that they are alert and aware of the here and now.

refocusing techniques A therapeutic process or technique used to limit tangential issues and to focus (refocus) the client's concentration to a specific set of therapeutic issues.

role-playing A therapeutic process that involves having the client play out various roles in order to deepen his or her insight and increase the patient's ability to see other peoples' points of view.

short-term goals A method of defining and measuring the intermediate steps the patient must take to achieve the treatment plan goal for discharge.

social support systems Significant people in the client's social environment who provide emotional and social feedback, opinions, responses, and help.

strengths Personal attributes like knowledge, interests, skills, aptitudes, and employment status, which may be useful in developing a meaningful treatment plan.

stressors Stimuli that the client perceives as stressful or that require excess energy to manage.

substantiated diagnosis The substantiated diagnosis evolves from the synthesis of assessment data from the various treatment disciplines; the primary focus of treatment.

suicidal contracts In a therapeutic setting the therapist has patients agree (either verbally or in writing) that they will not harm themselves for a period of time or during their therapy.

suicide attempt A specific action that has been taken by the client aimed at ending the client's life.

suicide gesture A suicide attempt in which the client intends to be discovered in order to influence or pressure the specific behavior of others.

surveyor An employee of an accrediting/credentialing body who performs a physical review of the patient's environment and treatment to ensure that the standards of the specific accrediting body are being met.

target symptoms The client's symptoms that are most likely to respond to treatment and therefore become the focus of therapeutic interventions.

T. B. D. To be done.

third party reimbursement Payment for health services by the government of other insurance carriers.

T. I. D. Ter in die (Latin for "three times a day," a prescription dosage).

treatment plan A plan created jointly by the treatment team and the patient which specifically outlines methods that will resolve problems and allow the patient to function at a higher level.

treatment plan update A report that outlines the patient's progress, or lack of progress, toward treatment goals and how the team intends to proceed with the patient's treatment.

utilization review A process of measuring the appropriateness of a patient's treatment and the need for continued stay.

V-Code A relational problem. Although it is not a psychiatric problem, it is intrusive enough to warrant primary attention during treatment.

voluntary admission An admission to a psychiatric hospital that requires the advance written consent of the patient to provide services, where the patient can choose to be discharged from care at a time of his or her choosing.

withdrawal The client's physiological and psychological response to the removal of a substance to which he or she is addicted.

References

Bersoff, D. N. (1999). *Ethical Conflicts in Psychology* (2nd ed.). Washington, DC: American Psychological Association.

Beutler, L., & M. Malik. (2002). *Rethinking the DSM*. Washington, DC: American Psychological Association.

Bjorck, J. P., J. Brown, & M. Goodman, (2000). *Casebook for Managing Managed Care: A Self-Study Guide for Treatment Planning, Documentation, and Communication*. Washington, DC: American Psychiatric Press.

Comprehensive Accreditation Manual for Behavioral Health Care 1999–2000. (1999). Oakbrook Terrace, IL: Joint Commission on Accreditation of Healthcare Organizations.

Comprehensive Accreditation Manual for Managed Behavioral Health Care (1st ed.) (1997). Oakbrook Terrace, IL: Joint Commission on Accreditation of Healthcare Organizations.

Cone, J. D. *Evaluating Outcomes: Empirical Tools for Effective Practice*. Washington, DC: American Psychological Association.

Desk Reference to the Diagnostic Criteria from DSM-IV-TR (4th ed.) (2000). Washington, DC: American Psychiatric Press.

Doenges, M. E. M., M. C. Townsend, & M. F. Moorhouse (1995). *Psychiatric Care Plans: Guidelines for Individualizing Care*, 3rd ed. Philadelphia: F. A. Davis.

DSM-IV-TR: Diagnostic and Statistical Manual of Mental Disorders (4th ed., rev.) (2000). Washington, DC: American Psychiatric Press.

Hamstra, B. (1994). *How Therapists Diagnose: Seeing Through the Psychiatric Eye*. Griffin, NY: St. Martin's.

Health Care Financing Administration (Provider Certification). (1995). *Conditions of Participation*, HCFA Pub. 7, Transmittal No. 276 Sept 1, 1995. State Operations Manual, Provider Certification.

Herlihy, B., & G. Corly (1997). *ACA Ethical Standards Casebook* (5th ed.). American Counseling Association.

Johnson, S. L. (1997). *Therapist's Guide to Clinical Intervention: The 1-2-3's of Treatment Planning*. San Francisco: Morgan Kaufmann.

Kaplan, Harold, MD, and Benjamin Sadock, MD. (1998). *Synopsis of Psychiatry: Behavioral Sciences/Clinical Psychiatry*. Philadelphia: Lippincott Williams & Wilkins.

Kattner, J. A., & R. Hayler (1997). *What You Never Learned in Graduate School*. New York: W. W. Norton.

Kennedy, J. A. (1995). *Fundamentals of Psychiatric Treatment Planning*. Washington, DC: American Psychiatric Press.

Kongstvredt, Peter R. (2002). *Managed Care: What It Is and How It Works* (2nd ed.). New York: Aspen Publishers.

Maxmen, J. S., & Ward, N. G. (1994). *Essential Psychopathology and Its Treatment Revised*. New York: W. W. Norton.

Morrison, J. (1995). *DSM-IV Made Easy*, Kitty Moore, ed. New York: Guilford Publications.

Professional Guide to Signs and Symptoms (3rd ed.). Springhouse, PA: Springhouse.

Quick Reference to the Diagnostic Criteria for the DSM-IV-TR. (2000). Washington, DC: American Psychiatric Press.

Shapiro, J. P., & D. K. Freedheim (1999). *The Clinical Child Documentation Sourcebook*. New York: Jossey-Bass.

Stuart, G. W. & M. T. Laraia (2001). *Principles and Practice of Psychiatric Nursing* (7th ed.). St. Louis: Mosby.

Index